Essential French Grammar

By

SEYMOUR RESNICK

Associate Professor of Romance Languages
Queens College

Dover Publications, Inc., New York

International Standard Book Number
ISBN-13: 978-0-486-20419-2
ISBN-10: 0-486-20419-7

Manufactured in the United States by Courier Corporation
20419738
www.doverpublications.com

Table of Contents

3

TABLE OF CONTENTS   7

Introduction

Essential French Grammar assumes that you will be spending a limited number of hours studying French grammar and that your objective is simple everyday communication. It is offered not as a condensed outline of all aspects of French grammar, but as a series of hints which will enable you to use more effectively and with greater versatility phrases and vocabulary that you have previously learned. You will become familiar with the more common structures and patterns of the language and learn a selected number of the most useful rules and forms.

How to Study Essential French Grammar

If you have studied French in a conventional manner, you will probably understand everything in *Essential French Grammar*, which can then serve as a refresher even though it uses a different approach than conventional grammars. You may want to glance through the book and then pay attention to those areas in which you are weak.

But if this is the first time you have studied French grammar, the following suggestions will be helpful.

1. Don't approach *Essential French Grammar* until you have mastered several hundred useful phrases and expressions such as you will find in any good phrase book or the *Listen & Learn* course. Everything will be more comprehensible and usable after you have achieved some simple, working knowledge of the language. The purpose of this book is to enable you to achieve greater fluency with the phrase approach, not to teach you to construct sentences from rules and vocabulary.

2. Read *Essential French Grammar* through at least once in its entirety. Don't be concerned if sections are not immediately clear to you; on

9

second or third reading, they will make better sense.   This first reading is necessary to give you a better understanding of certain terms and concepts used at the beginning.   What may appear discouragingly difficult at first will become more understandable as your studies progress.   As you use the language and hear it spoken, many aspects of French grammar will begin to form recognizable patterns.   *Essential French Grammar* will acquaint you with the structure and some of the peculiarities of the language, and will be helpful to you in developing your vocabulary and in generally improving your comprehension.

3. Go back to *Essential French Grammar* periodically.   Sections which seem difficult or of doubtful benefit to you now may prove extremely helpful later.

4. For the most part, *Essential French Grammar* is presented in a logical order, especially for the major divisions of grammar, and you will do best to follow its sequence in your studies.   However, the author is aware that some students learn best when they study to answer their immediate questions or needs (e.g., how to form the comparative; the conjugation of the verb *to be*, etc.).   If you prefer this approach, study entire sections, not only individual remarks.

5. Examples are given for every rule.   You may find it helpful to memorize the examples.   If you learn every example in this supplement and its literal translation, you will have been exposed to the most basic problems of French grammar and to models for their solution.

6. One cannot study French systematically without an understanding of its grammar, and the use and understanding of grammatical terms is as essential as a knowledge of certain mechanical terms when you learn to drive a car.   If your knowledge of grammatical terms is weak, read the Glossary of Grammatical Terms (p. 131) and refer to it whenever necessary.

There are many ways to express the same thought.   Every language has several different constructions to convey a single idea; some simple, others difficult. An involved verb conjugation may well be a more sophisticated way of expressing a thought and one which you may ultimately wish to master, but during your first experiments in communication you can achieve your aim by using a simple construction. Throughout this grammar you will find helpful hints on how to avoid difficult constructions.

As you begin to speak French, you will be your own best judge of the areas in which you need help in grammatical construction. If there is no one with whom to practice, speak mentally to yourself. In the course of a day see how many of the simple thoughts you've expressed in English can be stated in some manner in French. This kind of experimental self-testing will give direction to your study of grammar. Remember that you are studying this course in French not to pass an examination or receive a certificate, but to communicate with others on a simple but useful level. *Essential French Grammar* is not the equivalent of a formal course of study at a university. Although it could serve as a supplement to such a course, its primary aim is to help the adult study on his own. Indeed, no self-study or academic course or series could ever be offered that is ideally suited to every student. You must therefore rely on and be guided by your own rate of learning and your own requirements and interests.

If this grammar or any other grammar tends to inhibit your use of the language you may have learned through a simple phrase approach as taught in some schools and the *Listen & Learn* records, curtail your study of grammar until you feel it will really assist rather than hinder your speaking. Your objective is speaking, and you *can* learn to speak a language without formal grammatical training. The fundamental purpose of *Essential French Grammar* is to enable you to learn more rapidly and to eliminate hit and miss memorization. For those who prefer a more systematic approach, grammar does enable them to learn more quickly.

At the risk of being repetitious, the author must again urge you not to be afraid of making mistakes. The purpose of this grammar is not to teach you to speak like a native but to communicate and make yourself understood. If its goal is achieved, you will be speaking French and making mistakes rather than maintaining an inhibited silence. You will most certainly make errors in verb forms which are difficult for the English-speaking student to master, but don't let fear of errors deter you from speaking. *On apprend à parler en parlant*—One learns to speak by speaking. Sooner or later you'll review *Essential French Grammar* or a more detailed grammar at a time that is appropriate for polishing your speech.

Suggestions for Vocabulary Building

The following suggestions may be helpful to you in building your vocabulary:

1. Study words and word lists that answer real and preferably immediate personal needs. If you are planning to travel in the near future your motivation and orientation is clear cut and *Listen & Learn French* or a good travel phrase book will give you the material you need. Select material according to your personal interests and requirements. If you don't plan to motor, don't spend time studying the parts of the car. If you like foreign foods, study the supplementary foreign food list in *Listen & Learn French*. Even if you do not plan to travel in the near future, you will probably learn more quickly by imagining a travel or real life situation.

2. Use the association technique for memorization. For the most part, *Listen & Learn French* or travel phrase books give you associated word lists. If you continue to build your vocabulary by memorization, don't use a dictionary for this purpose. Select such grammars or books that have lists of word families.

3. Study the specialized vocabulary of your profession, business, or hobby. If you are interested in real estate, learn the many terms associated with property, buying, selling, leasing, etc. An interest in mathematics should lead you to a wide vocabulary in this science. Words in your specialty will be learned quickly and a surprising number will be applicable or transferable to other areas. Although these specialized vocabularies may not always be readily available, an active interest and a good dictionary will help you get started.

Abbreviations and Note

Abbreviations used in *Essential French Grammar*

MASC.	Masculine
FEM.	Feminine
SING.	Singular
PL.	Plural
LIT.	Literally
FAM.	Familiar
CONJ.	Conjugation
INFIN.	Infinitive
PART.	Participle
ADJ.	Adjective

Note: Whenever the French construction is basically different from the construction in English, a *literal* translation enclosed in brackets is given to help you analyze and understand the French syntax. This literal translation is immediately followed by a translation into idiomatic English.

Written Accents

There are three written accents which are placed on vowels in French. The most common is the acute accent (*l'accent aigu*) ´ which is used only over the vowel *e*. The *é* has the sound of English *a* as in ABC: *la vérité* (the truth), *parlé* (spoken).

The grave accent (*l'accent grave*) ` is used mainly over *e*, which then has the sound of *e* in *met*: *le père* (the father), *il lève* (he raises). The grave accent is also used over *a* and *u* (without affecting their pronunciation) in a few words to distinguish them from other words with the same spelling: *à* (to, at), *a* (has); *là* (there), *la* (the, it, her); *où* (where), *ou* (or).

The circumflex accent (*l'accent circonflexe*) ^ may be used over any vowel (â, ê, î, ô, û), and generally lengthens the sound of the vowel: *l'âge* (the age), *être* (to be), *l'île* (the isle), *le Rhône* (the Rhone River), *sûr* (sure).

The above accents do not indicate any special voice stress on the syllable where they occur.

The cedilla (*la cédille*) ، is placed under the letter *c* to give it the sound of *s* before *a*, *o* or *u*: *français* (French), *le garçon* (the boy, waiter), *reçu* (received).

Word Order

Normal word order

Word order in French is frequently the same as in English. Since many words in French are obviously related in appearance and derivation to English words, it is often easy to understand a French sentence even if you know only a minimum of grammar. Compare the following French sentences and their English translations:

Mon cousin et sa fiancée arrivent à six heures.
My cousin and his fiancee arrive at six o'clock.

La première leçon est très importante.
The first lesson is very important.

Negative Word Order*

To make a sentence negative, place *ne* before the verb and *pas* after it. (The *ne* becomes *n'* before a vowel or a silent *h*.)

Je *ne* parle *pas* très bien.
I do not speak very well.

Cette ville *n'*est *pas* très grande.
This city is not very large.

* See also page 78.

How to Form Questions

Three Common Question Forms

There are several ways of turning simple statements into questions in French.

1. The simplest way is to place *Est-ce que* in front of the original sentence. (The *que* becomes *qu'* if the next word begins with a vowel.) Study the following examples:

POSITIVE	INTERROGATIVE
Vous parlez anglais.	*Est-ce que* vous parlez anglais?
You speak English.	Do you speak English?
La cuisine est bonne ici.	*Est-ce que* la cuisine est bonne ici?
The food is good here.	Is the the food good here?
La première leçon est importante.	*Est-ce qu'*elle est importante?
	Is it (the lesson) important?
The first lesson is important.	

2. If the subject of the sentence is a second or third person pronoun—*vous* (you), *il* (he), *elle* (she), *ils* (they, MASC.), *elles* (they, FEM.)—the verb may be placed in front of the pronoun and joined to it by a hyphen.

Parlez-vous anglais?	*Est-elle* Américaine?
Do you speak English?	Is she American?
Est-il fatigué?	
Is he tired?	

However, if the verb ends in a vowel, a -*t*- must be inserted between the vowel and the third person singular pronouns (*il* and *elle*). This is done simply for ease of pronunciation.

Parle-*t*-il bien?   Va-*t*-elle aujourd'hui?
Does he speak well?   Is she going today?

3. A third common way of turning a simple statement into a question is by adding *n'est-ce pas?* to the end of the statement. This corresponds to the English phrases "isn't it?," "don't you?," "aren't we?," "won't you?," etc.

Paris est une ville intéressante, *n'est-ce pas?*
Paris is an interesting city, *isn't it?*

Vous resterez ici, *n'est-ce pas?*
You will stay here, *won't you?*

Interrogative Adjectives and Pronouns

The interrogative adjective "which" is translated by *quel* (MASC. SING.), *quelle* (FEM. SING.), *quels* (MASC. PL.) and *quelles* (FEM. PL.).   The corresponding pronouns (which one, which ones) are *lequel, laquelle, lesquels* and *lesquelles*.

The form of the adjective or pronoun used depends on the gender and number of the noun concerned.   For instance, in the first sentence below, *le livre* (the book) is a masculine singular noun, and the proper adjective and pronoun is, therefore, *quel* and *lequel*.   This concept of agreement of adjective and pronouns with nouns is further discussed on page 24.   See also the Glossary of Grammatical Terms on page 131.

Quel livre préférez-vous?   *Quelles* cravates préfèrent-ils?
Which book do you prefer?   *Which* ties do they prefer?

Lequel préférez-vous?   *Lesquelles* préfèrent-ils?
Which one do you prefer?   *Which ones* do they prefer?

Study the following explanations and examples of the other interrogative pronouns:

Qui translates both "who" and "whom," and may be used as subject or object, singular or plural, referring to persons:

Qui est là?   *Qui* avez-vous vu?
Who is there?   *Whom* did you see?

Qui is also used after prepositions, when referring to persons. Note that *à qui* translates "whose" (possession) as well as "to whom."

De qui parlez-vous?
Whom are you talking about?

À qui avez-vous donné la clé?
To whom did you give the key?

À qui est cette maison?
Whose house is this?

The interrogative "what" is translated as *qu'est-ce qui* when it is the subject of the sentence:

Qu'est-ce qui se passe?
What is going on?

"What" is translated as *que* or *qu'est-ce que* when it is an object:

Que désirez-vous? OR *Qu'est-ce que* vous désirez?
What do you wish?

Qu'est-ce que c'est?
What is it?

When asking for an explanation or a definition, "what is" is translated as *qu'est-ce que c'est que*:

*Qu'est-ce que c'est qu'*une république?
What is a republic?

Qu'est-ce que c'est que ça?
What is that?

"What," standing alone or when used as object of a preposition and not referring to persons , is *quoi*:

De *quoi* parliez-vous?   *Quoi?*
What were you talking about?   *What?*

Useful Interrogative Phrases

combien	how much	*comment*	how
quand	when	*où*	where
pourquoi	why		

Combien coûte ceci?
How much does this cost?

Comment va-t-on en ville?
How does one go to town?

Quand est-ce que l'autobus arrive?
When does the bus arrive?

Où est la gare?
Where is the station?

Pourquoi êtes-vous fâché?
Why are you angry?

Nouns and the Definite and Indefinite Articles

Gender of French Nouns

In French, all nouns are either masculine or feminine; there are no neuter nouns. Nouns denoting masculine persons or animals are of the masculine gender, and nouns denoting feminine persons or animals are of the feminine gender. However, this rule is no guide to the identification of the gender of the countless nouns which do not denote masculine or feminine persons or animals. The best way to learn the gender of these nouns is to memorize the definite article when you learn a new noun.

The Definite Article

In French, the definite article agrees in gender and number with the noun it accompanies. This is more complex than English in which one word, "the," serves as the proper definite article for all nouns. The forms of the French definite article are:

	MASC.	FEM.
SING.	le (l')	la (l')
PL.	les	les

Observations on the definite article:

1. *Les* is the only plural form of the definite article.

2. *L'* is used only with nouns which begin with a vowel or a silent h. For these nouns the indefinite article, discussed on p. 23, will serve as the guide to the identification of gender.

Plurals of Nouns

Regular Noun Plurals

Most French nouns form their plural by adding *-s* to the singular form.   (This *-s* is not pronounced.)

SING.	PL.
la capitale (the capital)	les capitale*s* (the capitals)
le mot (the word)	les mot*s* (the words)
l'arbre (the tree)	les arbre*s* (the trees)

Exceptions

1. Nouns whose singular ends in *-s*, *-x*, or *-z* remain unchanged in the plural.

SING.	PL.
le bra*s* (the arm)	les bra*s* (the arms)
la voi*x* (the voice)	les voi*x* (the voices)
le ne*z* (the nose)	les ne*z* (the noses)

2. Nouns ending in *-au* or *-eu* in the singular form their plural by adding *-x*.

SING.	PL.
le bure*au* (the office)	les bure*aux* (the offices)
le j*eu* (the game)	les j*eux* (the games)

3. Nouns whose singular ends in *-al* or *-ail* usually drop that ending and add instead *-aux* to form the plural.

SING.	PL.
le cheval	les chevaux
(the horse)	(the horses)
le travail	les travaux
(the work)	(the works)

4. Note the following very irregular cases:

SING.	PL.
l'œil	les yeux
(the eye)	(the eyes)
monsieur	messieurs
(sir, gentleman, Mr.)	(sirs, gentlemen)
madame	mesdames
(lady, madam, Mrs.)	(ladies, madams)
mademoiselle	mesdemoiselles
(young lady, miss)	(young ladies, misses)

The Indefinite Article

In English, the indefinite article is either "a" or "an." In French it is *un* before masculine nouns and *une* before feminine nouns.

MASC.	FEM.
un restaurant	*une* omelette
(a restaurant)	(an omelet)
un train	*une* cigarette
(a train)	(a cigarette)

As mentioned on page 21, the indefinite article will serve as a guide to the identification of gender of all nouns which begin with a vowel or with a silent h.

MASC.	FEM.
un homme	*une* heure
(a man)	(an hour)
un hôtel	*une* église
(an hotel)	(a church)

Adjectives

Agreement of Adjectives with Nouns

In French, adjectives agree in gender and in number with the nouns which they accompany. This is somewhat more complicated than in English where adjectives are invariable.

A French masculine singular noun requires the masculine singular form of all adjectives, and feminine plural nouns require feminine plural adjectives. Therefore, French adjectives have four forms—masculine singular, feminine singular, masculine plural, and feminine plural.

How to Form Feminine Singular Adjectives

The feminine singular adjective is normally formed by adding *-e* to the masculine singular form, unless the masculine singular form already ends in a silent *-e*, in which case the feminine singular form is identical to it.

In the examples, masculine adjectives are shown accompanying masculine nouns, and feminine adjectives agreeing with feminine nouns.

MASC. SING.	FEM. SING.
un grand pays (a great country)	une grande nation (a great nation)
un livre vert (a green book)	une robe verte (a green dress)
un jeune homme (a young man)	une jeune fille (a girl)
un garçon triste (a sad boy)	une histoire triste (a sad story)

24

FEMININE SINGULAR ADJECTIVES 25

Common Exceptions

MASC. SING. ending in	FEM. SING. changes to	Examples MASC.	FEM.	English
-eux	-euse	heur*eux*	heur*euse*	(happy)
-er	-ère	ch*er*	ch*ère*	(dear)
-el	-elle	natur*el*	natur*elle*	(natural)
-en	-enne	anci*en*	anci*enne*	(old, ancient)
-f	-ve	acti*f*	acti*ve*	(active)

Irregular Adjectives

The irregular feminine forms of the following common adjectives should be memorized:

MASC. SING.	FEM. SING.	ENG. MEANING
blanc	blanche	(white)
bon	bonne	(good)
doux	douce	(sweet)
faux	fausse	(false)
frais	fraîche	(fresh)
sec	sèche	(dry)

The following three adjectives, in addition to having irregular feminine forms, also have a secondary masculine form which is used before a masculine noun which begins with a vowel or a silent h. These adjectives are among the most common in the language and should be memorized.

MASC. SING.	MASC. SING (before vowel or mute h)	FEM. SING.	ENG. MEANING
beau	bel	belle	(beautiful)
nouveau	nouvel	nouvelle	(new)
vieux	vieil	vieille	(old)

Plurals of Adjectives

Most French adjectives form their plural similarly to the way in which noun plurals are formed, that is, by adding -s to the singular form.

MASC. SING.	MASC. PL.
le grand boulevard (the great boulevard)	les grands boulevards (the great boulevards)
le chapeau vert (the green hat)	les chapeaux verts (the green hats)

FEM. SING.	FEM. PL.
la grande nation (the great nation)	les grandes nations (the great nations)
la robe verte (the green dress)	les robes vertes (the green dresses)

Common Exceptions

1. If the masculine singular form ends in -s or -x, there is no change in the masculine plural.

MASC. SING.	MASC. PL.
un chapeau *gris* (a gray hat)	deux chapeaux *gris* (two gray hats)
Il est *vieux*. (He is old.)	Ils sont *vieux*. (They are old.)

2. Adjectives ending in *-eau* form their masculine plural by adding *-x*.

MASC. SING.	MASC. PL.
le *beau* jour (the beautiful day)	les b*eaux* jours (the beautiful days)
un nouv*eau* train (a new train)	deux nouv*eaux* trains (two new trains)

Placement of Adjectives

French descriptive adjectives normally follow the nouns they modify.   Note that this is contrary to normal English usage.

un restaurant français   une langue difficile
(a French restaurant)   (a difficult language)

les pays importants   les robes bleues
(the important countries)   (the blue dresses)

The following is a list of common French adjectives which normally *precede* the nouns they modify.   As they are very frequently used, one should become familiar with all their forms and with their correct position in the sentence.   You will note that we have already studied the various forms of most of them.

MASC. SING.	MASC. PL.	FEM. SING.	FEM. PL.	ENG. MEANING
beau (bel*)	beaux	belle	belles	(beautiful)
bon	bons	bonne	bonnes	(good)
cher	chers	chère	chères	(dear)
gentil	gentils	gentille	gentilles	(nice)
grand	grands	grande	grandes	(big, great)
jeune	jeunes	jeune	jeunes	(young)
joli	jolis	jolie	jolies	(pretty)
long	longs	longue	longues	(long)
mauvais	mauvais	mauvaise	mauvaises	(bad)
meilleur	meilleurs	meilleure	meilleures	(better, best)
nouveau (nouvel*)	nouveaux	nouvelle	nouvelles	(new)
petit	petits	petite	petites	(little)
vieux (vieil*)	vieux	vieille	vieilles	(old)

Examples:

un beau village   une longue histoire
(a beautiful village)   (a long story)

* Usage of this secondary masculine singular form is explained on page 25.

une bonne amie
(a good friend (fem.))

les chères tantes
(the dear aunts)

les gentils garçons
(the nice boys)

un grand parc
(a large park)

les jeunes sœurs
(the young sisters)

une jolie robe
(a pretty dress)

le mauvais temps
(the bad weather)

mon meilleur ami
(my best friend)

les nouveaux livres
(the new books)

le petit café
(the little café)

une vieille voiture
(an old car)

Adverbs

How to Form Adverbs in French

In English, we often form adverbs by adding -*ly* to an adjective, as, for instance, in the case of clear, clear*ly*; polite, polite*ly*. Adverbs are commonly formed in French in much the same way, except that the ending added to the adjective is -*ment*. This is added to the masculine singular form of the adjective, provided that that form ends in a vowel. If it does not end in a vowel, the -*ment* is added to the feminine singular adjective.

MASC. SING. ADJ.	ENG. MEANING	FEM. SING. ADJ.*
poli	(polite)	—
facile	(easy)	—
parfait	(perfect)	parfaite
naturel	(natural)	naturelle
malheureux	(unhappy)	malheureuse

ADVERB	ENG. MEANING
poliment	(politely)
facilement	(easily)
parfaitement	(perfectly)
naturellement	(naturally)
malheureusement	(unhappily)

Adverbs in French are invariable, that is, they do not change endings to agree in gender and number with the subject of the sentence. Adverbs in French generally follow the verb they modify.

Je suis *vraiment* enchanté d'être en France.
I am *really* delighted to be in France.

Je comprends *parfaitement* quand vous parlez *lentement*.
I understand *perfectly* when you speak *slowly*.

* The feminine singular form of the adjective is given only in the cases where the masculine singular form does not end in a vowel.

Verbs

Comparison of English and French Verbs

English verbs are rather simple to learn. They require very few changes of endings, and the ones which are required are relatively uniform. For example, the present tense of the verb "to sing" is: I sing; you sing; he, she, it sing*s*; we sing; you (PL.) sing; they sing.

French verbs are more complex. French verbs require more endings which vary according to the person and number of the subject. There are three main types of verbs or conjugations, and most verbs may be used correctly by following the model or sample verb for that conjugation. The three conjugations are:

		MODEL VERB
1ST CONJ.	verbs whose infinitive* ends in *-er*	*parler* (to speak)
2ND CONJ.	verbs whose infinitive ends in *-ir*	*finir* (to finish)
3RD CONJ.	verbs whose infinitive ends in *-re*	*vendre* (to sell)

The great majority of French verbs belong to the 1st conjugation and, with very few exceptions, the verbs in this conjugation are regular, that is, they take endings or are conjugated exactly the way the model verb *parler* is conjugated.

The Present Tense

Comparison of Present Tense in French and English

Although we are usually not aware of it, in English we have three different ways of expressing an action in the present. We

---

* The infinitive is the form of the verb which corresponds to "to sing," "to be," "to have," "to know," etc. If you are not clear on this point, see the Glossary of Grammatical Terms.

can say "I walk," or (progressive) "I am walking," or (emphatic) "I do walk." There are slight shades of meaning which distinguish these forms. In French, however, there is only one way of expressing an action in the present, and this one way conveys all the meanings of the three English constructions.

1st Conjugation Verbs (Infinitive ending -er)

parler (to speak)

je parl*e*	I speak, am speaking
tu parl*es*	you (FAM. SING.) speak, are speaking
il (elle) parl*e*	he (she) speaks, is speaking
nous parl*ons*	we speak, are speaking
vous parl*ez*	you speak, are speaking
ils (elles) parl*ent*	they speak, are speaking

Several points should be noted:

1. The *tu* form is the familiar singular, used only to address close friends, close relatives (such as members of one's family), children, and animals. A tourist will probably have no occasion to use this form and should always use *vous*, which can refer to both singular and plural subjects, the same as the pronoun "you" in English.

2. All the singular forms and the third person plural (*je parle, tu parles, il parle, ils parlent*) are pronounced alike.

3. The first person plural (the *nous* form) of all verbs of all conjugations and in all tenses, with only one exception (*nous sommes*, we are), ends in *-ons*.

4. The *vous* form of all verbs in all tenses, with very few exceptions, ends in *-ez*.

5. The third person plural (*ils* and *elles*) form of all verbs in all tenses without exception ends in *-nt*.

2nd Conjugation Verbs (Infinitive ending -ir)

finir (to finish)

je fin*is*	I finish, am finishing
tu fin*is*	you finish, are finishing
il (elle) fin*it*	he (she) finishes, is finishing
nous fin*issons*	we finish, are finishing
vous fin*issez*	you finish, are finishing
ils (elles) fin*issent*	they finish, are finishing

Notes on the second conjugation:

1. All the singular forms (*je finis, tu finis, il finit*) are pronounced alike.

2. The plural endings are the same as for the 1st conjugation (*-ons, -ez, -ent*) except that *-iss-* is placed before them.

3. There are not many verbs that follow the pattern of *finir*. The following are the most important and probably the only ones a tourist is likely to need:

bâtir (to build)	remplir (to fill)
choisir (to choose)	réussir (to succeed)

4. Two common verbs ending in -*ir* are conjugated like 1st conjugation verbs.

ouvrir (to open)   offrir (to offer)

j'ouvr*e*	nous ouvr*ons*	j'offr*e*	nous offr*ons*
tu ouvr*es*	vous ouvr*ez*	tu offr*es*	vous offr*ez*
il (elle) ouvr*e*	ils (elles) ouvr*ent*	il (elle) offr*e*	ils (elles) offr*ent*

5. A number of important verbs ending in -*ir* are irregular and are discussed in the irregular verb section, p. 34.

3rd Conjugation Verbs (Infinitive ending -re)

vendre (to sell)

je vend*s*	I sell, am selling
tu vend*s*	you sell, are selling
il (elle) vend	he (she) sells, is selling

nous vend*ons*	we sell, are selling
vous vend*ez*	you sell, are selling
ils (elles) vend*ent*	they sell, are selling

Notes on the third conjugation:

1. All the singular forms are pronounced alike (*je vends, tu vends, il vend*).

2. The plural endings are the same as for the 1st conjugation (*-ons, -ez, -ent*).

3. There are not many verbs that follow exactly the pattern of *vendre*. The following are the most important:

attendre	(to wait for)	perdre	(to lose)
défendre	(to forbid, defend)	rendre	(to give back)
descendre	(to descend)	répondre	(to answer)
entendre	(to hear)	rompre*	(to break)

4. A number of important *-re* verbs are irregular and are discussed in the irregular verb section which follows.

---

* The *il* (*elle*) form of this verb is *rompt*.

The Present Tense of Common Irregular Verbs

The following irregular verbs are so frequently used that the student will do well to memorize their forms.

INFINITIVE	je	tu	il, elle	nous	vous	ils, elles
aller (to go)	vais	vas	va	allons	allez	vont
avoir (to have)	ai	as	a	avons	avez	ont
boire (to drink)	bois	bois	boit	buvons	buvez	boivent
connaître* (to know)	connais	connais	connaît	connaissons	connaissez	connaissent
courir (to run)	cours	cours	court	courons	courez	courent
croire (to believe)	crois	crois	croit	croyons	croyez	croient
devoir (must, ought)	dois	dois	doit	devons	devez	doivent
dire (to say)	dis	dis	dit	disons	dites	disent
dormir (to sleep)	dors	dors	dort	dormons	dormez	dorment
écrire (to write)	écris	écris	écrit	écrivons	écrivez	écrivent
être (to be)	suis	es	est	sommes	êtes	sont
faire (to do, make)	fais	fais	fait	faisons	faites	font

lire (to read)	lis	lis	lit	lisons	lisez	lisent
mettre† (to put)	mets	mets	met	mettons	mettez	mettent
mourir (to die)	meurs	meurs	meurt	mourons	mourez	meurent
pouvoir (to be able)	peux	peux	peut	pouvons	pouvez	peuvent
partir (to leave)	pars	pars	part	partons	partez	partent
prendre‡ (to take)	prends	prends	prend	prenons	prenez	prennent
recevoir (to receive)	reçois	reçois	reçoit	recevons	recevez	reçoivent
savoir (to know)	sais	sais	sait	savons	savez	savent
servir (to serve)	sers	sers	sert	servons	servez	servent
sortir (to go out)	sors	sors	sort	sortons	sortez	sortent
suivre (to follow)	suis	suis	suit	suivons	suivez	suivent
venir§ (to come)	viens	viens	vient	venons	venez	viennent
voir (to see)	vois	vois	voit	voyons	voyez	voient
vouloir (to wish, want)	veux	veux	veut	voulons	voulez	veulent

* *Reconnaître* (to recognize) is conjugated like *connaître.*
† *Permettre* (to permit) and *promettre* (to promise) are conjugated like *mettre.*
‡ *Apprendre* (to learn) and *comprendre* (to understand) are conjugated like *prendre.*
§ *Devenir* (to become) and *revenir* (to come back) are conjugated like *venir.*

The Command or Imperative Form

How to Form Commands

The command form ("Speak!") is the *vous* form of the present tense of the verb without the subject pronoun.

Parlez!	(Speak!)	Descendez!	(Come down!)
Choisissez!	(Choose!)	Dites!	(Say! Tell!)

The command is usually softened by adding *s'il vous plaît* (please).

> Parl*ez* plus haut, s'il vous plaît.
> Speak louder, please.

> Descend*ez* vite, s'il vous plaît.
> Come down quickly, please.

How to Avoid the Command Form

A substitute for the command form is the use of the *vous* form of the verb *vouloir* (to wish, want) plus the infinitive of the working verb in the normal question word order (see rule 2, page 17). The word *bien* is often inserted after the word *vous* to soften the statement. This construction is equivalent to the English phrase "Will you please . . . ?"

> Voulez-vous (bien) parlez plus haut?
> Will you please speak louder?

> Voulez-vous (bien) laisser la clé?
> Will you please leave the key?

First Person Plural Commands

The first person plural command "Let's speak!" is the present tense of the verb without the subject pronoun *nous*.

All*ons*!	(Let's go!)	Lis*ons*!	(Let's read!)
Bât*issons*!	(Let's build!)	Ouvr*ons*!	(Let's open!)

Irregular Command Forms

The verb *être* (to be) has irregular command forms:

Soyez ici à quatre heures.   *Be* here at four o'clock.
Soyons heureux.   *Let's be* happy.

The *Passé Composé* or Past Indefinite Tense

Comparison of the Past Indefinite Tense in French and English

French, like English, has several ways of expressing a past event. The past tense which is most important and most useful in French is called *le passé composé*. It corresponds to the English simple past (I spoke, I finished, I bought) as well as to the English present perfect (I have spoken, I have finished, I have bought).

How to Form the *Passé Composé* and the Past Participle

The *passé composé* of most verbs is formed by using the present tense of the verb *avoir* (to have) and the past participle. This is very similar to the way in which the present perfect tense in English is formed. The past participle ends in *-é* for the first conjugation verbs (parler, parl*é*), in *-i* for the second conjugation verbs (finir, fin*i*), and in *-u* for the third conjugation verbs (vendre, vend*u*).

Study the following models:

1ST CONJ. VERBS
(*visiter*—to visit)

j'ai visité	I visited, have visited
tu as visité	you visited, have visited
il (elle) a visité	he (she) visited, has visited
nous avons visité	we visited, have visited
vous avez visité	you visited, have visited
ils (elles) ont visité	they visited, have visited

2ND CONJ. VERBS
(*choisir*—to choose)

j'ai choisi	I chose, have chosen
tu as choisi	you chose, have chosen
il (elle) a choisi	he (she) chose, has chosen
nous avons choisi	we chose, have chosen
vous avez choisi	you chose, have chosen
ils (elles) ont choisi	they chose, have chosen

3RD CONJ. VERBS
(*perdre*—to lose)

j'ai perdu	I lost, have lost
tu as perdu	you lost, have lost
il (elle) a perdu	he (she) lost, has lost
nous avons perdu	we lost, have lost
vous avez perdu	you lost, have lost
ils (elles) ont perdu	they lost, have lost

Verbs with Irregular Past Participles

INFINITIVE	PAST PARTICIPLE
s'asseoir (to be seated)	assis (seated)
avoir (to have)	eu (had)
boire (to drink)	bu (drunk)
conduire (to conduct)	conduit (conducted)
connaître (to know)	connu (known)
courir (to run)	couru (run)
croire (to believe)	cru (believed)
devoir (to owe; must)	dû (ought)
dire (to say, tell)	dit (said, told)
être (to be)	été (been)
écrire (to write)	écrit (written)
faire (to do, make)	fait (done, made)
lire (to read)	lu (read)
mettre (to put)	mis (put)
mourir (to die)	mort (died)

INFINITIVE	PAST PARTICIPLE
naître (to be born)	né (born)
offrir (to offer)	offert (offered)
ouvrir (to open)	ouvert (opened)
partir (to leave)	parti (left)
pouvoir (to be able)	pu (been able)
prendre (to take)	pris (taken)
recevoir (to receive)	reçu (received)
rire (laugh)	ri (laughed)
savoir (to know)	su (known)
venir (to come)	venu (come)
voir (to see)	vu (seen)
vouloir (to wish, want)	voulu (wished, wanted)

How to Use the *Passé Composé*

Study the following sentences which contain examples of the past tense:

Nous avons dépensé beaucoup d'argent.
We spent (have spent) a lot of money.

J'ai déjà *reçu* l'invitation.
I have already *received* the invitation.

Elle a été malade la semaine dernière.
She was ill last week.

Verbs Which Form Their Compound Tenses Using *être* as the Auxiliary Verb

The following sixteen verbs use *être* and not *avoir* as the auxiliary verb to form the *passé composé* and other compound tenses.*

aller (to go)	entrer (to enter)
arriver (to arrive)	monter (to go up)
descendre (to descend)	mourir (to die)
devenir (to become)	naître (to be born)

* Reflexive verbs are also conjugated with *être* in the past indefinite and other compound tenses. See p. 51.

partir (to leave)	revenir (to come back)
rentrer (to return)	sortir (to go out)
rester (to remain)	tomber (to fall)
retourner (to return)	venir (to come)

The past participle of verbs conjugated with *être* as the auxiliary verb change endings so as to agree in gender and number with the subject of the verb. If the subject is feminine singular, an -*e* is added to the past participle. If the subject is masculine plural, a -*s* is added, and if it is feminine plural an -*es* is added. (These changes do not affect pronunciation, however, except in the case of the verb *mourir*, past participle: *mort, morts, morte, mortes*. The addition of the -*e* in the feminine singular and plural forms causes the *t* to be sounded.)

Study the conjugation of the verb *sortir* in the *passé composé*. Observe the changes which the past participle makes in order to agree in gender and number with the subject.

sortir (to leave, go out)

je suis sorti	I (MASC.) left, have left
je suis sortie	I (FEM.) left, have left
tu es sorti	you (MASC. FAM.) left, have left
tu es sortie	you (FEM. FAM.) left, have left
il est sorti	he left, has left
elle est sortie	she left, has left
nous sommes sortis	we (MASC. PL. or MASC. and FEM. PL.) left, have left
nous sommes sorties	we (FEM. PL.) left, have left
vous êtes sorti	you (MASC. SING.) left, have left
vous êtes sortie	you (FEM. SING.) left, have left
vous êtes sortis	you (MASC. PL. or MASC. and FEM. PL.) left, have left
vous êtes sorties	you (FEM. PL.) left, have left
ils sont sortis	they (MASC. PL. or MASC. and FEM. PL.) left, have left
elles sont sorties	they (FEM. PL.) left, have left

Ils *sont arrivés* hier et *sont allés* tout de suite au consulat américain.
They *arrived* yesterday and *went* at once to the American consulate.

Nous *sommes restés* longtemps.
We *stayed* a long time.

How to Use *ne . . . pas* with Compound Tenses

To make a sentence negative in the *passé composé* or any other compound tense, surround the auxiliary verb (*avoir* or *être*) by *ne . . . pas.* (Remember that *ne* contracts to *n'* before a vowel.)

Je *n'ai pas* encore payé la note.
I *haven't* paid the bill yet.

Elles *ne sont pas* arrivées à temps.
They (FEM.) *did not* arrive on time.

How to Form Questions in Compound Tenses

To make a sentence involving a compound tense negative, either use *est-ce que* as in the present tense (see p. 17), or place the auxiliary verb before the subject and connect it to the subject by a hyphen. Note that a *-t-* is inserted in the third person singular of verbs conjugated with *avoir*.

Est-ce que vous avez commencé le roman?
Have you begun the novel?

or

Avez-vous commencé le roman?
Have you begun the novel?

Est-ce qu'il a bien travaillé?
Did he work well?

or

A-t-il bien travaillé?
Did he work well?

*Est-ce qu'*elle est rentrée de bonne heure?
Did she come back early?

or

Est-elle rentrée de bonne heure?
Did she come back early?

The Imperfect Tense

How to Form the Imperfect Tense

Another past tense in French is the imperfect. It is used to express what *was happening* or what *used to happen*. It is formed by dropping the *-ons* of the first person plural of the present tense (nous parl-ons, nous finiss-ons, nous attend-ons), and adding the following endings:

(je)	*-ais*	(nous)	*-ions*
(tu)	*-ais*	(vous)	*-iez*
(il, elle)	*-ait*	(ils, elles)	*-aient*

Study the following models:

1ST CONJ. VERBS
(*parler*—to speak)

je parl*ais*	I spoke, used to speak, was speaking
tu parl*ais*	you spoke, used to speak, were speaking
il (elle) parl*ait*	he (she) spoke, used to speak, was speaking
nous parl*ions*	we spoke, used to speak, were speaking
vous parl*iez*	you spoke, used to speak, were speaking
ils (elles) parl*aient*	they spoke, used to speak, were speaking

2ND CONJ. VERBS
(*finir*—to finish)

je finiss*ais*	I finished, used to finish, was finishing
tu finiss*ais*	you finished, used to finish, were finishing
il (elle) finiss*ait*	he (she) finished, used to finish, was finishing
nous finiss*ions*	we finished, used to finish, were finishing
vous finiss*iez*	you finished, used to finish, were finishing
ils (elles) finiss*aient*	they finished, used to finish, were finishing

43

3RD CONJ. VERBS
(*attendre*—to wait)

j'attend*ais*	I waited, used to wait, was waiting
tu attend*ais*	you waited, used to wait, were waiting
il (elle) attend*ait*	he (she) waited, used to wait, was waiting
nous attend*ions*	we waited, used to wait, were waiting
vous attend*iez*	you waited, used to wait, were waiting
ils (elles) attend*aient*	they waited, used to wait, were waiting

Observations about the imperfect:

1. All the singular forms and the third person plural (*-ais, -ais, -ait, -aient*) are pronounced alike.

2. The endings of the first and second persons plural (*-ions, -iez*) are the same as in the present tense except for the insertion of the *i* before the ending.

3. The only irregular verb in the imperfect tense is *être* (to be). *Être* uses the stem *ét-*, to which the regular imperfect endings are added (j'ét*ais*, tu ét*ais*, il (elle) ét*ait*, nous ét*ions*, vous ét*iez*, ils (elles) ét*aient*).

How to Use the Imperfect Tense

The following sentences will show you the difference between the imperfect and the *passé composé*. Note that the imperfect describes actions which *used to happen*, repeatedly or regularly, or actions which *were taking place* when something else happened. The *passé composé*, on the other hand, is used to describe single rather than repeated actions, and generally actions which are considered completed.

I *used to see* him every day.
Je le *voyais* tous les jours. (*imperfect*)
I *saw* him yesterday.
Je l'*ai vu* hier. (*passé composé*)
What *were you doing* when he *called* you?
Que *faisiez*-vous (*imperfect*) quand il vous *a téléphoné*? (*passé composé*)

What *did you do* when he *called* you?

Qu'*avez-vous fait* (*passé composé*) quand il vous *a téléphoné?* (*passé composé*)

I *did not have* a lot of money when I *was* young.

Je *n'avais pas* (*imperfect*) beaucoup d'argent quand j'*étais* (*imperfect*) jeune.

Certain verbs which by their very nature express an attitude or a condition rather than an action, use the imperfect more frequently than the *passé composé*. The following are the most important:

avoir	(to have)	être	(to be)
croire	(to believe)	penser	(to think)
désirer	(to desire, want)	pouvoir	(to be able)
espérer	(to hope)	savoir	(to know)
		vouloir	(to want, wish)

Il *croyait* que nous *n'avions pas* l'argent.

He *thought* we *did not have* the money.

Je *voulais* la voir.

I *wanted* to see her.

Je *ne savais pas* s'ils *pouvaient* venir.

I *didn't know* if they *could* come.

The Pluperfect Tense

The pluperfect tense (in English, *had* plus the past participle) in French is formed with the imperfect of *avoir* (or *être* for the verbs which are conjugated with *être* [see p. 39]) and the past participle. The French pluperfect corresponds in usage to English. It is not extremely important for a beginner since the *passé composé* will convey the meaning adequately.

Study the following models:

(prendre—to take)

j'avais pris	I had taken
tu avais pris	you had taken

il (elle) avait pris	he (she) had taken
nous avions pris	we had taken
vous aviez pris	you had taken
ils (elles) avaient pris	they had taken

(*tomber*—to fall)

j'étais tombé (tombée*)	I had fallen
tu étais tombé (tombée)	you had fallen
il était tombé	he had fallen
elle était tombée	she had fallen
nous étions tombés (tombées)	we had fallen
vous étiez tombé (tombée) (tombés) (tombées)	you had fallen
ils étaient tombés	they had fallen
elles étaien: tombées	they had fallen

Here are some examples of the usage of the pluperfect tense.

Je n'*avais* jamais *été* en Europe.
I *had* never *been* to Europe.

Elle *était partie* avant leur arrivée.
She *had left* before their arrival.

The Future Tense

The Future Tense of Regular Verbs

The future tense (in English, *will* or *shall* plus the infinitive) is formed in French by adding the following endings to the infinitive form of the verb:

(je)	-*ai*	(nous)	-*ons*
(tu)	-*as*	(vous)	-*ez*
(il, elle)	-*a*	(ils, elles)	-*ont*

* Remember that the past participle of verbs conjugated with *être* changes endings to show agreement in gender and number with the subject of the sentence. Therefore, *tombé* is the masculine singular form, *tombée* the feminine singular form, *tombés* the masculine plural form, and *tombées* the feminine plural form. See page 40 for further discussion of this point of grammar.

Study the following models, and notice that 3rd conjugation verbs drop the final -e of the infinitive before the future endings are attached.

1ST CONJ. VERBS
(*donner*—to give)

je donner*ai*	I shall give
tu donner*as*	you will give
il (elle) donner*a*	he (she) will give
nous donner*ons*	we shall give
vous donner*ez*	you will give
ils (elles) donner*ont*	they will give

2ND CONJ. VERBS
(*bâtir*—to build)

je bâtir*ai*	I shall build
tu bâtir*as*	you will build
il (elle) bâtir*a*	he (she) will build
nous bâtir*ons*	we shall build
vous bâtir*ez*	you will build
ils (elles) bâtir*ont*	they will build

3RD CONJ. VERBS
(*rendre*—to give back)

je rendr*ai*	I shall give back
tu rendr*as*	you will give back
il (elle) rendr*a*	he (she) will give back
nous rendr*ons*	we shall give back
vous rendr*ez*	you will give back
ils (elles) rendr*ont*	they will give back

The Future Tense of Irregular Verbs

All verbs, both regular and irregular, use the endings given above to form the future tense, but with the following important verbs these endings are added to irregular stems, instead of to the infinitive. You should become familiar with these irregular futures.

INFINITIVE	je	tu	il, elle	nous	vous	ils, elles
aller(to go)	irai	iras	ira	irons	irez	iront
avoir (to have)	aurai	auras	aura	aurons	aurez	auront
devoir (must, ought)	devrai	devras	devra	devrons	devrez	devront
envoyer (to send)	enverrai	enverras	enverra	enverrons	enverrez	enverront
être (to be)	serai	seras	sera	serons	serez	seront
faire (to do, make)	ferai	feras	fera	ferons	ferez	feront
pouvoir (to be able)	pourrai	pourras	pourra	pourrons	pourrez	pourront
recevoir (to receive)	recevrai	recevras	recevra	recevrons	recevrez	recevront
savoir (to know)	saurai	sauras	saura	saurons	saurez	sauront
venir (to come)	viendrai	viendras	viendra	viendrons	viendrez	viendront
voir (to see)	verrai	verras	verra	verrons	verrez	verront
vouloir (to want, wish)	voudrai	voudras	voudra	voudrons	voudrez	voudront

How to Use the Future Tense

Study the following sentences illustrating the use of the future, which corresponds in general to English:

Qu'est-ce que vous *ferez* demain?
What *will* you *do* tomorrow?

Nous *reviendrons* de bonne heure parce que nous *irons* au théâtre le soir.
We *shall return* early because we *shall go* to the theater in the evening.

Quand *partirez*-vous pour Nice?
When *will* you *leave* for Nice?

How to Avoid the Future Tense

It is often correct to use the present tense instead of the future tense, sometimes indicating the idea of future action by such words as "next week," "tomorrow," etc.

Qu'est-ce que vous *faites demain?*
What *are* you *doing* (will you do) *tomorrow?*

Je *pars* pour Nice *lundi.*
I *leave* (shall leave) for Nice on *Monday.*

In English we often say "I am going to go," instead of "I shall go." Similarly, in French, one may use the present tense of the verb *aller* (to go) plus the infinitive of the other verb.

Qu'est-ce que vous *allez faire?*
What are you *going to do?*

Je *vais étudier*, et après je *vais me reposer* un peu.
I am *going to study*, and afterwards I am *going to rest* a little.

The Conditional Tenses

How to Form the Conditional Tense

The conditional tense is expressed in English by the word

"would" plus the infinitive (e.g. I would go, they would come). The past conditional is expressed by the words "would have" plus the past participle (e.g. She would have answered, we would have seen).

To form the conditional in French, we add the endings of the imperfect tense (*-ais, -ais, -ait, -ions, -iez, -aient*) to the entire infinitive of first and second conjugation verbs, but to the infinitive minus the final *-e* of third conjugation verbs.

(manger—to eat)

je manger*ais*	I would eat
tu manger*ais*	you would eat
il (elle) manger*ait*	he (she) would eat
nous manger*ions*	we would eat
vous manger*iez*	you would eat
ils (elles) manger*aient*	they would eat

Irregular Verbs

Verbs that have an irregular stem in the future (see p. 47) have the same stem for the conditional:

INFINITIVE	CONDITIONAL
aller (to go)	j'irais (I would go)
avoir (to have)	j'aurais (I would have)
devoir (must, ought)	je devrais (I ought)
envoyer (to send)	j'enverrais (I would send)
être (to be)	je serais (I would be)
faire (to do, make)	je ferais (I would make, would do)
pouvoir (to be able)	je pourrais (I would be able)
recevoir (to receive)	je recevrais (I would receive)
savoir (to know)	je saurais (I would know)
venir (to come)	je viendrais (I would come)
voir (to see)	je verrais (I would see)
vouloir (to want, wish)	je voudrais (I would want, would like)

How to Form the Past Conditional Tense

To form the past conditional, use the conditional of *avoir* (or *être* with the special *être* verbs, listed on page 39), plus the past participle. Remember that the past participle of verbs conjugated with *être* agrees in gender and number with the subject (see p. 40).

(acheter—to buy)

j'aurais acheté	I would have bought
tu aurais acheté	you would have bought
il (elle) aurait acheté	he (she) would have bought
nous aurions acheté	we would have bought
vous auriez acheté	you would have bought
ils (elles) auraient acheté	they would have bought

(revenir—to return, come back)

je serais revenu (*fem.* revenue)	I would have returned
tu serais revenu (*fem.* revenue)	you would have returned
il serait revenu	he would have returned
elle serait revenue	she would have returned
nous serions revenus (*fem.* revenues)	we would have returned
vous seriez revenue (*fem. sing.* revenue) (*masc. pl.* revenus) (*fem. pl.* revenues)	you would have returned
ils seraient revenus	they would have returned
elles seraient revenues	they would have returned

How to Use the Conditional Tenses

Here are some sentences containing conditionals and past conditionals:

Je *voudrais* parler avec le gérant.
I *would like* to speak with the manager.

Si j'avais assez d'argent, j'*irais* en Italie.
If I had enough money, I *would go* to Italy.

Je n'*aurais* jamais *fait* cela.
I *would* never *have done* that.

Nous *serions arrivés* à temps si elle n'*était* pas *venue* en retard.
We *would have arrived* on time if she *had* not *come* late.

In the second sentence, note that when we use the conditional (*j'irais*) in the main clause, the imperfect (*j'avais*) is used in the *si* or "if" clause.   In the last sentence, we use the past conditional (*nous serions arrivés*) in the main clause and the pluperfect (*elle était venue*) in the *si* ("if") clause.

Reflexive Verbs

Comparison of Reflexive Verbs in English and French

In English we say: I get up, I wash, I shave, I dress.   The action of each of these verbs refers back to the subject, and these phrases might also be expressed: I get *myself* up, I wash *myself*, I shave *myself*, I dress *myself*.   In French these verbs are reflexive verbs and must be used with special reflexive pronouns:

me* (myself, to or for myself)
te* (yourself, to or for yourself)
se* (himself, herself, itself, themselves, to or for himself, herself, itself, themselves)
nous (ourselves, to or for ourselves)
vous (yourself, yourselves, to or for yourself, yourselves)

In French, the phrases given in the first paragraph of this section would be: Je *me* lève, je *me* lave, je *me* rase, je *m*'habille.

The infinitive of reflexive verbs is preceded by the reflexive pronoun *se* (or, if the verb begins with a vowel or silent *h*, by *s*'): *se* lever (to get up), *se* laver (to wash), *s*'habiller (to dress), etc.

Conjugation of Reflexive Verbs

All reflexive verbs form their compound tenses using *être* as the auxiliary verb.   The reflexive pronoun is placed immediately

* *Me, te, se* become *m', t' s'* before a vowel or silent *h*.

in front of the verb itself, except in affirmative commands, when it follows the verb to which it is attached by a hyphen.

The typical reflexive verb *se dépêcher* (to hurry) will serve to illustrate the conjugation of a reflexive verb in its most important tenses.

PRESENT TENSE

(*se dépêcher*—to hurry)

je me dépêche	I hurry
tu te dépêches	you hurry
il (elle) se dépêche	he (she) hurries
nous nous dépêchons	we hurry
vous vous dépêchez	you hurry
ils (elles) se dépêchent	they hurry

PASSÉ COMPOSÉ TENSE

je me suis dépêché (*fem.* dépêchée)	I hurried
tu t'es dépêché (*fem.* dépêchée)	you hurried
il s'est dépêché	he hurried
elle s'est dépêchée	she hurried
nous nous sommes dépêchés (*fem.* dépêchées)	we hurried
vous vous êtes dépêché (*fem. sing.* dépêchée)	
(*masc. pl.* dépêchés) (*fem. pl.* dépêchées)	you hurried
ils se sont dépêchés	they hurried
elles se sont dépêchées	they hurried

FUTURE TENSE

je me dépêcherai	I shall hurry
tu te dépêcheras	you will hurry
il (elle) se dépêchera	he (she) will hurry
nous nous dépêcherons	we shall hurry
vous vous dépêcherez	you will hurry
ils (elles) se dépêcheront	they will hurry

COMMAND FORM

Dépêchez-vous!	Hurry!
Ne vous dépêchez pas!	Don't hurry!
Dépêchons-nous!	Let's hurry!
Ne nous dépêchons pas!	Let's not hurry!

Important Reflexive Verbs

Reflexive verbs are far more popular in French than in English. Here is a list of the practically indispensable ones:

s'amuser (to have a good time)
s'appeler (to be called, named)
s'asseoir (to sit down)
se coucher (to go to bed)
se dépêcher (to hurry)
s'habiller (to get dressed)
se laver (to wash)
se lever (to get up)
se porter (to be, feel [health])
se raser (to shave)
se taire (to be quiet)
se trouver (to be located)

Most reflexive verbs may also be used without reflexive pronouns. For example, *laver* means "to wash (someone or something)," *appeler* means "to call (someone or something)," *raser* means "to shave (someone)," etc.

How to Use Reflexive Verbs

Study the following sentences, which further illustrate the use of reflexive verbs:

Le coiffeur ne m'a pas bien rasé. (*not refl.*)
The barber did not shave me well.

Je me rase tous les jours. (*refl.*)
I shave every day.

Je vais appeler Henri. (*not refl.*)
I am going to call Henry.

Je m'appelle Georges. (*refl.*)
My name is George.

Asseyez-vous ici, s'il vous plaît. (*refl.*)
Sit down here, please.

Je me lave les mains et la figure avant de m'habiller.
(*refl*).
I wash my hands and face before dressing.

The Passive Voice

How to Form the Passive Voice

The passive in English (*to be* with a past participle) is usually similarly formed in French with the auxiliary verb *être* plus the past participle. This construction occurs most frequently in the *passé composé* (use *passé composé* of *être* plus past participle) and future (use future of *être* plus past participle).

> Ces lettres *ont été écrites** par mon frère.
> These letters *were written* by my brother.
>
> Un grand édifice *sera construit* ici par le gouvernement.
> A tall building *will be constructed* here by the government.

The English passive sometimes expresses an indefinite idea, such as: *it is said* that he is rich, meaning "people say," "one says," "they say." In such cases, French does not use the passive construction, but rather the popular pronoun *on* (one) and the active form of the verb.

---

* As discussed on page 40, the past participle of verbs conjugated with the auxiliary verb *être* agrees in gender and number with the subject of the sentence.

On dit qu'il est riche.	*On parle* anglais ici.
[*One says* that he is rich.]	[*One speaks* English here.]
It is said that he is rich.	English *is spoken* here.

Occasionally the English passive is translated by a reflexive in French:

Cela ne *se fait* pas.
[That *does* not *do itself*.]
That *is* not *done*.

The Present Participle

In French, the present participle is formed by adding *-ant* to the stem of the first person plural of the present tense: nous parlons, parl*ant*; nous finissons, finiss*ant*; nous vendons, vend*ant*.

In English we often use the present participle after a preposition, as in phrases like "before leaving," "after eating," "without thinking." The only preposition in French which is followed by the present participle is *en* (on, upon, while, by):

en entrant (upon entering)
en voyageant (while traveling, by traveling)

All other prepositions are followed by the *infinitive* form of the verb:

avant de partir (before leaving)
pour travailler (in order to work)
sans parler (without speaking)

Prepositions and Infinitives

Some French verbs require the preposition *à* or *de* before a following infinitive, while others are followed by the infinitive directly without an intervening preposition. You will no doubt have noticed this while listening to your *Listen & Learn* course. Become familiar with the most popular verbs given below, and the preposition they require, if any, before an infinitive.

Verbs Which Require *à* before the Infinitive

Some of the most frequently used verbs which require the preposition *à* before an infinitive are:

apprendre (to learn)
aider (to help)
enseigner (to teach)

commencer (to begin)
inviter (to invite)

Here are some sentences using the above verbs:

Nous *apprenons à* lire et *à* écrire.
We *are learning* to read and write.

Il m'*enseigne à* nager.
He *is teaching* me to swim.

Il nous *a invités à* dîner chez lui.
He *invited* us to dine at his house.

Nous *commençons à* comprendre.
We *are beginning* to understand.

Je vous *aiderai à* le faire.
I *shall help* you do it.

Verbs Which Require *de* before the Infinitive

The following verbs are among the most common which require the preposition *de* before an infinitive:

cesser (to stop)
décider (to decide)
défendre (to forbid)
demander (to ask)
dire (to tell)
empêcher (to prevent)
essayer (to try)

tâcher (to try)
se garder (to take care not to)
manquer (to fail)
oublier (to forget)
promettre (to promise)
refuser (to refuse)
se souvenir (to remember)

Study the following models:

Est-ce qu'il *a cessé de* pleuvoir?
Has it *stopped* raining?

Il est *défendu de* faire cela.
It is *forbidden* to do that.

Ne *manquez* pas *d'*y aller.
Don't *fail* to go there.

Je me *garderai de* le lui dire.
I *shall be careful not* to tell it to him.

Il a promis qu'il *tâcherait de* venir.
He promised that he *would try* to come.

Verbs Followed Directly by the Infinitive

Many verbs in French are followed by the infinitive form of the
verb and do not use either *à* or *de*. The most important are:

vouloir (to want, wish)	savoir (to know how to)
désirer (to want, desire)	pouvoir (to be able to, can)
aimer (to like)	il faut (it is necessary)
aimer mieux (to prefer)	compter (to intend)
préférer (to prefer)	oser (to dare)
aller (to be going to)	laisser (to let, allow)
devoir (must, ought)	envoyer (to send)

Examine the following examples:

Je *compte revenir* ici l'année prochaine.
I *intend to come back* here next year.

Nous ne *voulons* pas le *faire*.
We *do* not *want to do* it.

Laissez-moi *parler*.
Let me *speak*.

Envoyez chercher le médecin.
Send for the doctor.

Je n'*oserais* pas *aller* si loin si je ne *savais* pas *nager*.
I *would*n't *dare* (*to*) *go* so far if I did not *know how to swim*.

The Subjunctive

Though little used in English, the subjunctive is frequent and important in French. We are presenting briefly its formation and main uses, primarily for recognition when you see it or hear it rather than for active use.

The Present Subjunctive

The present subjunctive for most verbs is formed by taking the third person plural (the *ils* and *elles* form) of the present indicative (pp. 30–33), dropping the *-ent*, and adding *-e*, *-es*, *-e*, *-ions*, *-iez*, *-ent*:

INFINITIVE	3RD PERS. PL.	PRESENT SUBJUNCTIVE
parler (to speak)	parl*ent*	parl*e*, parl*es*, parl*e*, parl*ions*, parl*iez*, parl*ent*
finir (to finish)	finiss*ent*	finiss*e*, finiss*es*, finiss*e*, finiss*ions*, finiss*iez*, finiss*ent*
vendre (to sell)	vend*ent*	vend*e*, vend*es*, vend*e*, vend*ions*, vend*iez*, vend*ent*

The following important verbs, although using the standard endings, do not follow the rule. When one is first beginning to speak French, it is probably best not to try to memorize these forms, but only to become familiar with them so that one recognizes them when one hears them.

aller (to go)	aille, ailles, aille, allions, alliez, aillent
faire (to do, make)	fasse, fasses, fasse, fassions, fassiez, fassent
pouvoir (to be able)	puisse, puisses, puisse, puissions, puissiez, puissent
prendre (to take)	prenne, prennes, prenne, prenions, preniez, prennent
recevoir (to receive)	reçoive, reçoives, reçoive, recevions, receviez, reçoivent

| savoir (to know) | sache, saches, sache, sachions, sachiez, sachent |
| venir (to come) | vienne, viennes, vienne, venions, veniez, viennent |

The Past Subjunctive

The past subjunctive, for a completed action, is formed by using the present subjunctive of *avoir* or *être* (see p. 39 for *être* verbs) before the past participle of the main verb:

PAST. SUBJ. OF AN "AVOIR VERB"		PAST SUBJ. OF AN "ÊTRE VERB"	
j'aie		je sois	
tu aies		tu sois	
il (elle) ait		il (elle) soit	
nous ayons	parlé	nous soyons	entré(e)(s)*
vous ayez		vous soyez	
ils (elles) aient		ils (elles) soient	

Uses of the Subjunctive

The main uses of the subjunctive are as follows:

1. After the verb "to want" (*vouloir, désirer*) when there is a change of subject in the subordinate clause:

> Je veux que vous le *fassiez*.
> [I want that you *do* it.]
> I want you *to do* it.

But not when the subject is the same:

> Je veux *faire* ceci.
> I want *to do* this.

2. After expressions of emotion (*regretter*, to be sorry; *être content*, to be glad; *être surpris*, to be surprised; etc.):

---

* The past participles of verbs conjugated with *être* change endings to agree in gender and number with the subject of the verb. (See p. 40.)

Nous sommes surpris qu'elle *ait dit* cela.
We are surprised that she *said* that.

Je regrette qu'ils *soient partis.*
I am sorry that they *left.*

3. After the verb "to doubt" (*douter*):

Je doute qu'il le *sache.*
I doubt that he *knows* it.

4. After certain impersonal expressions (*il faut,* it is necessary; *il est possible,* it is possible; etc.):

Il faut que vous y *alliez* ce soir.
[It is necessary that you *go* there this evening.]
You must *go* there this evening.

5. After certain conjunctions (*bien que* or *quoique,* although; *pour que,* so that; *avant que,* before; *pourvu que,* provided; etc.):

Dites-moi tout avant qu'il *vienne.*
Tell me everything before he *comes.*

Personal Pronouns

In French, as in English, pronouns* have different forms according to their use or position in a sentence. We have already seen many times in the Verb Section the subject pronouns (*je, tu, il, elle, nous, vous, ils, elles*) and the reflexive pronouns (*me, te, se, nous, vous, se*). We shall now take up the other important pronoun forms.

Direct and Indirect Object Pronouns

The English object pronouns (me, you, him, her, it, us, them) are either direct (He·takes *it*) or indirect (He gives *me* the book, or, He gives the book *to me*).† In French, the object pronouns are as follows:

DIRECT	INDIRECT
me (me)	me (to me)
te (you)	te (to you)
le (him, it *masc.*)	lui (to him, her, it)
la (her, it *fem.*)	
nous (us)	nous (to us)
vous (you)	vous (to you)
les (them)	leur (to them)

Their normal position is before the verb. However, in an affirmative command they follow the verb and are attached to it by a hyphen, just as we have seen with the reflexive pronouns (page 51). Study the following sentences:

* If you are not clear as to what a pronoun is, refer to the Glossary of Grammatical Terms.

† The difference between direct and indirect objects is further explained in the Glossary of Grammatical Terms.

Ils *m*'ont donné l'argent.
They gave *me* the money.

Elle *l*'a trouvé.
She found *it*.

Je *lui* ai expliqué le problème.
I explained the problem *to him*.

Je ne *la* vois pas maintenant, mais je *lui* ai parlé il y a quelques
   minutes.
I don't see *her* now, but I spoke *to her* a few minutes ago.

Dites-*moi* la vérité.
Tell *me* the truth.

Ne *me* dérangez pas.
Don't bother *me*.

Observations on direct and indirect object pronouns:

1. The singular object pronouns (*me, te, le, la*) become *m', t',* and *l'* before a word beginning with a vowel.

2. In a negative sentence, the *ne* comes before the object pronoun, the *pas* is in its usual position after the verb.

3. The *me* becomes *moi* when attached to the verb (in the affirmative command).

Sequence of Pronouns

When there are two object pronouns, the following order is observed in most cases:

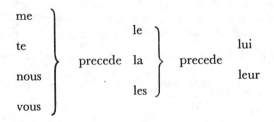

Nous *le lui* avons donné.
We gave *it to him.*

Il *me l'*a dit.
He told *it to me.*

In an affirmative command, however, the *le, la* and *les* come between the verb and the indirect object.

Donnez-*les-moi.*   Give *them to me.*
Apportez-*le-leur.*   Bring *it to them.*

How to Avoid Difficult Pronoun Constructions

If you find the double object construction somewhat complicated, try to avoid it in this way. Instead of saying, "We gave it to him" (*Nous le lui avons donné*), say "We gave the book to him" (*Nous lui avons donné le livre*) or "We gave it to John" (*Nous l'avons donné à Jean*). In other words, eliminate one of the object pronouns and substitute a noun. It is even possible to avoid the object pronouns entirely in some cases by saying "We gave the book to John" (*Nous avons donné le livre à Jean*).

Prepositional Forms of the Personal Pronouns

The pronouns used after prepositions are known technically as disjunctive personal pronouns. They are: *moi, toi, lui, elle, nous, vous, eux, elles.* Study the following examples:

contre *moi*	against *me*	entre *nous*	among *us*
avec *toi*	with *you*	pour *vous*	for *you*
de *lui*	from *him*	devant *eux*	in front of *them*
sans *elle*	without *her*	chez *elles*	at their house (at the home of *them*)

The prepositional form of the personal pronoun is also used when it stands alone without a verb.

Qui sait la réponse? *Moi.*
Who knows the answer? *I* (do).

Table of Personal Pronouns

The following table will be a useful reference in reviewing the personal pronouns. The familiar singular forms (*tu*) have been placed in parentheses to help remind you that you rarely need to use them. As has been pointed out on page 31, these forms are generally reserved for addressing close friends and close relatives, children, and animals.

SUBJECT	REFLEXIVE	DIRECT	INDIRECT	PREPOSITIONAL
je	me	me	me	moi
(tu)	(te)	(te)	(te)	(toi)
il	se	le	lui	lui
elle	se	la	lui	elle
nous	nous	nous	nous	nous
vous	vous	vous	vous	vous
ils	se	les	leur	eux
elles	se	les	leur	elles

Expressing Possession

Comparison of Possessives in English and French

In English, you can say either "the teacher's book" or "the book of the teacher." There is no form corresponding to the apostrophe *s* in French to express possession. Instead a form comparable to "the book of the teacher" is used.

le palais du roi
[the palace of the king]
the king's palace

les rues de Paris
the streets of Paris

la plume de ma tante
[the pen of my aunt]
my aunt's pen

la chambre de Marie
[the room of Mary]
Mary's room

Possessive Adjectives

The French possessive adjectives are as follows:

MASC. SING.	FEM. SING.*	MASC. & FEM. PL.	ENGLISH
mon	ma	mes	(my)
ton	ta	tes	(your [*fam.*])
son	sa	ses	(his, her, its)
notre	notre	nos	(our)
votre	votre	vos	(your)
leur	leur	leurs	(their)

These words, like other adjectives, agree in number and gender with the nouns they modify. Thus, *son père* may mean *his father* or *her father*, and *sa sœur* may mean *his sister* or *her sister*.

* Before vowels, the forms *mon, ton, son* are used.

Je cherche *mon* passeport.
I am looking for *my* passport.

Où sont *nos* valises?
Where are *our* valises?

Quelle est *votre* adresse?
What is *your* address?

Elle cherche *son* frère.
She is looking for *her* brother.

Expressing Possession after the Verb *être*

The usual way of showing ownership after the verb *être* (to be), is to use *à* plus the prepositional form of the pronoun.

à moi	(mine)	à nous	(ours)
à toi	(yours)	à vous	(yours)
à lui	(his)	à eux	(theirs *masc.*)
à elle	(hers)	à elles	(theirs *fem.*)

Cette place est *à moi*.
This seat is *mine*.

Ces papiers sont *à nous*.
These papers are *ours*.

We may also express ownership after *être* by using the proper form of the possessive pronoun, given in the following table.

MASC. SING.	FEM. SING.	MASC. PL.	FEM. PL.	ENGLISH
le mien	la mienne	les miens	les miennes	(mine)
le tien	la tienne	les tiens	les tiennes	(yours)
le sien	la sienne	les siens	les siennes	(his, hers)
le nôtre	la nôtre	les nôtres	les nôtres	(ours)
le vôtre	la vôtre	les vôtres	les vôtres	(yours)
le leur	la leur	les leurs	les leurs	(theirs)

Cette place est *la mienne*.
This seat is *mine*.

Ces papiers sont *les nôtres.*
These papers are *ours.*

It should be pointed out that this construction is more emphatic than the use of *à moi,* etc., discussed above.

Contraction of *à* or *de* and the Definite Article

The prepositions *à* (to, at) and *de* (from, of) combine with the definite articles *le* and *les* as follows:

à + *le* becomes *au*	*de* + *le* becomes *du*
à + *les* becomes *aux*	*de* + *les* becomes *des*

There is no contraction of *à* or *de* plus *la* or *l'*.

J'ai envoyé un télégramme *au* président *du* pays.
I sent a telegram *to the* president *of the* country.

Je vais *aux* États-Unis.
I am going *to the* United States.

La couleur *des* maisons était rouge.
The color *of the* houses was red.

Il a perdu la balle *de l'*enfant.
He lost the child'*s* ball.

The Partitive Construction

Comparison between French and English

In English we frequently say: "Do you want coffee?" or "We have bananas and apples." The words "some" or "any" are understood in these sentences (i.e. "Do you want *some* coffee?", "We have *some* bananas," etc.). French requires the partitive construction, which means that the words "some" or "any" must be expressed.

How to Use the Partitive Construction

"Some" or "any" are represented in French by the preposition *de* plus the form of the definite article which agrees in gender and number with the noun which follows. Therefore, before a masculine singular noun the proper expression would be *du*; before a feminine singular noun, *de la*; before a masculine or feminine singular noun which begins with a vowel or silent *h*, *de l'*; before a masculine or feminine plural noun, *des*.

Voulez-vous *du* café?
Do you want (*some, any*) coffee?

Nous avons *des* bananes et *des* pommes.
We have (*some*) bananas and (*some*) apples.

There are several cases where *de* alone (without the article) is required. The most important of these to remember is negative sentences.

POSITIVE	NEGATIVE
Nous avons *du* fromage.	Nous n'avons pas *de* fromage.
We have (*some*) cheese.	We don't have *any* cheese.
Il y a *des* poires.	Il n'y a pas *de* poires.
There are (*some*) pears.	There aren't *any* pears.
Elle a *des* amis ici.	Elle n'a pas *d'*amis ici.
She has (*some*) friends here.	She hasn't *any* friends here.

Demonstrative Adjectives and Pronouns

Demonstrative Adjectives

In French "this" and "that" are expressed by the following words: *ce, cet,* and *cette.* "These" and "those" are expressed by the word *ces.*

Study the following examples:

ce crayon
this (or *that*) pencil
cette école
this (or *that*) school
ces hôtels
these (or *those*) hotels

cet hôtel
this (or *that*) hotel
ces crayons
these (or *those*) pencils
ces écoles
these (or *those*) schools

Observations on the demonstrative adjectives:

1. *Ce* is the normal word for "this" and "that" to be used before masculine singular nouns.

2. *Cet* is used before masculine nouns which begin with a vowel or a silent *h.*

3. *Cette* is used before all feminine singular nouns.

4. *Ces* is used before all plural nouns.

Emphatic Forms of the Demonstrative Adjectives

If you wish to emphasize or make a contrast between *this* or *that, these* or *those,* add *-ci* (for *this* and *these*) or *-là* (for *that* and *those*) to the end of the noun.

ce crayon-*ci*
this pencil

ces écoles-*ci*
these schools

ce crayon-*là*
that pencil

ces écoles-*là*
those schools

Demonstrative Pronouns

The demonstrative pronoun *celui* (the one, this one, that one) changes to agree in gender and number with the noun for which it stands. Its forms are:

MASC. SING.	FEM. SING.	MASC. PL.	FEM. PL.
celui	celle	ceux	celles

How to Use the Demonstrative Pronouns

These words are not used by themselves, but are always followed by (1) a prepositional phrase; (2) a relative clause; or (3) the particle *-ci* or *-là*, used for emphasis or contrast.

1. Ce livre et *celui* de ma mère sont verts.
   This book and *the one* of my mother are green.
2. Notre voiture est *celle* qui est dans le garage.
   Our car is *the one* which is in the garage.
3. Voulez-vous ce chapeau-ci? Non, je préfère *celui-là*.
   Do you want this hat? No, I prefer *that one*.

Neuter Demonstrative Pronouns

The neuter demonstrative pronouns *ceci* and *cela* translate *this* and *that* respectively. *Cela* is frequently contracted into *ça*.

Study the usage of these words in the following examples. Note that *ceci*, *cela*, and *ça* usually refer to an idea or indefinite concept.

Ceci n'est pas trop difficile.
This is not too difficult.

Cela ne me plaît pas.
I do not like *that*.

Qu'est-ce que c'est que *ça*?
What's *that*?

Ça suffit.
That is enough.

C'est *ça*.
That's it; *that*'s right.

Comparisons of Adjectives and Adverbs

How to Form the Comparative of Adjectives and Adverbs

In English, we have two ways of changing adjectives and adverbs from positive to comparative degree.   Many of our most common adjectives and adverbs are changed by adding -er to them, i.e.: rich, rich*er*; soon, soon*er*.   Other adjectives and adverbs are made comparative by placing the words "more" (or "less") in front of them, i.e.: beautiful, *more* beautiful; slowly, *more* slowly, *less* slowly.

In French, comparatives are formed by placing *plus* (or *moins*) in front of the adjective or adverb, i.e.: riche, *plus* riche; vite, *plus* vite, *moins* vite.

How to Use the Comparative in French

Elle est *plus jolie* que sa sœur.
She is *prettier* than her sister.

Vous parlez *plus vite* que lui.
You speak *faster* than he (does).

Ce village est *moins intéressant* que celui que nous avons visité la semaine dernière.
This village is *less interesting* than the one we visited last week.

Jean est *aussi intelligent que* son frère.
Jean is *as intelligent as* his brother.

Parlez *aussi lentement que* moi.
Speak *as slowly as* I (do).

Observations on the uses of the comparative:

1. In comparatives, "than" is translated by *que*.
2. In French, a comparison of equality (as . . . as) is expressed by *aussi . . . que*.

73

Miscellaneous Comparative Expressions

Before nouns, "more" is translated as *plus de*, and "as much," "as many" are translated by *autant de*. "So much," "so many" are rendered by *tant de*.

La Côte d'Azur a *plus de touristes* que la Bretagne.
The Riviera has *more tourists* than Brittany.

Il y a *autant de voitures* ici qu'à Paris.
There are *as many cars* here as in Paris.

Nous avons encore *tant de choses* à faire!
We still have *so many things* to do!

The Superlative

The superlative degree is expressed in English by adding -est to an adjective or adverb (i.e.: rich, rich*est*, soon, soon*est*), or by placing the words "most" or "least" in front of the adjective or adverb (i.e.: beautiful, *most* beautiful; slowly, *most* slowly, *least* slowly).

The superlative in French is expressed by placing the definite article and the words *plus* or *moins* in front of the adjective or adverb.

Je crois que c'est la région *la plus pittoresque* du pays.
I think that it is *the most picturesque* region in the country.

Pierre est *le plus grand* élève de la classe.
Peter is *the tallest* pupil in the class.

Jean lit *le plus vite*.
John reads *the fastest*.

Observations on the superlative:

1. The form of the definite article (*le, la, les*) used depends upon the noun which follows, to which the adjective refers and with which it agrees in gender and number. However, the article is always *le* in *adverbial* superlative expressions.

2. The word "in" after a superlative expression is translated as *de*.

Irregular Comparative and Superlative Forms

The comparative and superlative forms of the adjective *bon* (good) and the comparative of the adverb *bien* (well) are irregular in both languages:

	POSITIVE	COMPARATIVE	SUPERLATIVE
ADJECTIVE	bon (good)	meilleur (better, *masc.*)	le meilleur (the best, *masc.*)
		meilleure (better, *fem.*)	la meilleure (the best, *fem.*)
ADVERB	bien (well)	mieux (better)	le mieux (the best)

Si nous allions à un *meilleur* restaurant, nous mangerions *mieux*.

If we went to a *better* restaurant, we would eat *better*.

The Relative Pronouns *Qui* and *Que*

The most important relative pronouns in French are *qui* (*who*, *that*, *which*), used as subject, and *que* (*whom*, *that*, *which*), used as object. Both *qui* and *que* may refer to persons or things, singular or plural. The following sentences illustrate their uses. Note that *que* becomes *qu'* before a vowel, but *qui* does not change.

> L'homme *qui* vous attendait est sorti.
> The man *who* was waiting for you has left.

> L'homme *que* vous attendez n'est pas encore arrivé.
> The man (*whom*) you are waiting for has not yet arrived.

> Voici un dictionnaire *qui* vous aidera beaucoup.
> Here is a dictionary *which* will help you a great deal.

> Je ne trouve pas le café *qu'*il m'a recommandé.
> I do not find the café (*that*) he recommended to me.

Notice in the above translations that in English we may omit the relative pronoun when used as object (*whom*, *that*, *which*). In French this is never permitted, and the *que* must be expressed. We must also point out that *que* is also the equivalent of the conjunction *that*, often omitted in English, but always included in French.

> Il m'a dit *qu'*il ne pouvait pas venir.
> He told me (*that*) he could not come.

Compound Relative Pronouns

The relative *what* is translated as *ce qui* when used as subject, and *ce que* when used as object.

Dites-moi *ce qui* est arrivé.
Tell me *what* happened.

Il nous a dit *ce qu*'il savait.
He told us *what* he knew.

Negative Expressions

As pointed out on page 16, we can make sentences negative by placing *ne* before the verb and *pas* after it. A number of other negatives may be used in the place of *pas*. The following are the most important:

ne . . . rien   (nothing, anything)
ne . . . jamais   (never)
ne . . . personne   (no one, nobody)

Il *ne* m'a *rien* dit.
He did*n't* tell me *anything*.

Je *ne* fume *jamais*.
I *never* smoke.

Nous *ne* voyons *personne*.
We do *not* see *anyone*.

Rien, jamais and *personne* may also be used alone.

Qu'avez-vous dit? *Rien.*
What did you say? *Nothing.*

Avez-vous été en Suisse? *Jamais.*
Have you been in Switzerland? *Never.*

Qui est là? *Personne.*
Who is there? *No one..*

Idiomatic Verbs

There are a number of frequently used verbs which are extremely useful and require special discussion. The most important of these verbs have been selected, and idiomatic expressions formed with them are illustrated in the following pages.

Aller (to go)

Aller is very important as the verb used for greeting and inquiring about one's health.

Comment allez-vous?
[How go you?]
How are you?

Comment ça va? (more popular and familiar)
[How it goes?]
How are you?

Ça va.
[It goes.]
Fine; O. K.

Je vais très bien, merci.
[I go very well, thanks.]
I'm very well, thank you.

Study also the following expressions which use the verb *aller*.

Nous allons à pied.   (*aller à pied*—to walk, LIT.: to go on
We walk.   foot)

Cette robe vous va bien.
[This dress goes you well.]
This dress looks well on you.

79

Allons donc!
[Let's go then!]
Come, now!

Ça va sans dire.
That goes without saying.

Remember also that the present tense of *aller* plus infinitive is a handy substitute for the future, as discussed on page 48.

Je vais le faire demain.
I am going to (shall) do it tomorrow.

Ils ne vont pas commencer jusqu'à mon retour.
They are not going to (will not) begin until my return.

Avoir (to have)

In addition to its important function as an auxiliary verb used in the formation of compound tenses, the very basic verb *avoir* (to have) is used in many special constructions.

To be hungry, thirsty, warm, cold, etc. are rendered in French as to *have hunger, thirst, warmth, cold,* etc.

avoir chaud (to be warm)
  J'ai chaud.
  [I have warmth.]
  I am warm.

avoir froid (to be cold)
  Il a froid.
  [He has cold.]
  He is cold.

avoir faim (to be hungry)
  Nous avons faim.
  [We have hunger.]
  We are hungry.

avoir peur (to be afraid)
  Avez-vous peur?
  [Have you fear?]
  Are you afraid?

avoir raison (to be right)
  Qui a raison?
  [Who has right?]
  Who is right?

avoir tort (to be wrong)
  Ils ont tort.
  [They have wrong.]
  They are wrong.

avoir soif (to be thirsty)
   Elles ont soif.
   [They have thirst.]
   They are thirsty.

avoir sommeil (to be sleepy)
   J'ai sommeil.
   [I have sleep.]
   I am sleepy.

Note also the following idioms:

   Qu'avez-vous?
   [What have you?]
   What is the matter with you?

   La conférence aura lieu ce soir.
   The lecture will take place this
   evening.

avoir mal à l'estomac (to have a stomach ache)
   J'ai mal à l'estomac (à la tête, aux dents).
   [I have ill to the stomach (to the head, to the teeth).]
   I have a stomach ache (headache, toothache).

avoir besoin de (to need)
   J'ai besoin de mon stylo.
   [I have need of my pen.]
   I need my pen.

avoir envie de (to feel like)
   J'ai envie de dormir toute la
   journée.
   [I have desire to sleep all day.]
   I feel like sleeping all day.

avoir de la chance (to be lucky)
   Vous avez de la chance.
   [You have luck.]
   You are lucky.

Age is expressed by *avoir* followed by the number of years:

   Quel âge avez-vous?
   [What age have you?]
   How old are you?

   J'ai vingt-huit ans.
   [I have twenty-eight years.]
   I am twenty-eight years old.

The useful expression *il y a* means both *there is* and *ago*:

   Il n'y a pas d'eau sur la table.
   There is no water on the table.

   Qu'est-ce qu'il y a?
   [What is there?]
   What is the matter?

Il est sorti il y a cinq minutes.
He left five minutes ago.

Do not confuse *il y a* with *voilà* (there is, there are), used when you point out something.

Voilà l'Hôtel de Ville.
There is the City Hall.

Note also *voici* (here is, here are):

Voici mes papiers.
Here are my papers.

Me voici.
Here I am.

Devoir (**to owe; must, ought**)

The basic meaning of *devoir* is "to owe."

Qu'est-ce que je vous *dois*?
What do I *owe* you?

It is also used (with a following infinitive) to express obligation. The conditional (*je devrais*) is milder and more polite than the present (*je dois*).

Je *dois* partir tout de suite.
I *must* leave at once.

Vous *devriez* la voir avant de partir.
You *should* see her before leaving.

J'*aurais dû* la voir.
I *ought to have* seen her.

Devoir also expresses supposition, inference, probability.

Vous *devez être* fatigué après votre voyage.
You *must be* (*probably are*) tired after your trip.

Il *doit être* malade.
He *must be* (*probably is*) sick.

Être (**to be**)

The verb *être* (to be) has been discussed on pages 39 and 51 as the auxiliary verb used in the formation of compound tenses of certain verbs and of all reflexive verbs. It is also used in the following important idiomatic expressions:

être de retour (to be back)
    Je serai de retour à neuf heures.
    I shall be back at nine o'clock.

être en retard (to be late)
    J'espère que le train ne sera pas en retard.
    I hope the train won't be late.

être sur le point de (to be about to)
    Nous étions sur le point de sortir.
    We were about to leave.

être en train de (to be in the act of)
    Nous sommes en train de le décider.
    We are (in the act of) deciding it.

être enrhumé (to have a cold)
    Marie est enrhumée et ne pourra pas nous accompagner.
    Mary has a cold and will not be able to accompany us.

Note also :
    Ce n'est pas la peine.
    It is not worth the effort.

The verb *être* is also used to tell time in French. Its usage in expressions of time is discussed on page 88.

Faire (**to make, do**)

In addition to being one of the most common verbs in the language, *faire* (to do, make) is also used in a variety of idiomatic expressions. Most expressions of weather in French use *faire*.

Quel temps fait-il?	Il fait chaud.
[What weather makes it?]	[It makes warm.]
How is the weather?	It's warm.
Il fait beau (temps).	Il fait froid.
[It makes good (weather).]	[It makes cold.]
The weather is fine.	It's cold.
Il fait mauvais (temps).	Il fait du vent.
[It makes bad (weather).]	[It makes some wind.]
The weather is bad.	It's windy.
Il fait doux.	Il fait du soleil.
[It makes mild.]	[It makes some sun.]
It's mild.	It's sunny.

Other common expressions using the verb *faire*:

Cela ne fait rien.	Cela ne me fait rien.
That doesn't matter.	I don't care.

faire un voyage (to take a trip)
  J'aimerais faire un voyage.
  I would like to take a trip.

faire une promenade (to take a walk)
  Nous faisons une promenade.
  We take a walk.

faire des emplettes (to go shopping)
  Je dois faire des emplettes cet après-midi.
  I must go shopping this afternoon.

faire mal (to hurt, be painful)
  Est-ce que cela vous fait mal?
  Does that hurt you?

Falloir (**to be necessary**)

The verb *falloir* (to be necessary) is used only in the third person singular form, and usually occurs either in the present (*il faut*) or future (*il faudra*) tenses. It is generally followed by an infinitive, and is translated as "one must," "one should," "one ought," "it is necessary," or, in the future, as "one will have to," "it will be necessary," etc. The verb *devoir* discussed on page 82, expresses a similar idea.

Il faut étudier pour apprendre.
It is necessary to (one must) study in order to learn.

Il faudra passer au moins quinze jours en Provence.
It will be necessary to spend at least two weeks in Provence.

Penser (**to think**)

"To think of, or about" a person or thing is expressed by *penser à*, but if we mean "to have an opinion of" we must use *penser de*.

À quoi pensez-vous?	Je pense *à* mes amis.
What are you thinking about?	I am thinking of my friends.
À qui pensez-vous?	Que pensez-vous *de* mes amis?
Whom are you thinking about?	What do you think of my friends?

Savoir (**to know**) and *Connaître* (**to meet, be acquainted with**)

In English, we use the same verb, "to know," for both knowing facts and knowing people. In French, however, these ideas are separated. *Savoir* means to know facts, to have information, to know how to. *Connaître* means to know or be acquainted with persons and places.

Savez-vous ce qu'il a dit?
Do you know what he said?

Je voudrais *savoir* tout ce qui s'est passé.
I would like to know everything that happened.

Est-ce qu'elle *sait* nager?
Does she know how to swim?

Je *connais* ce monsieur mais je ne *sais* pas son nom.
I know that gentleman but I don't know his name.

Connaissez-vous Bruxelles?
Are you acquainted with Brussels?

Note the expression *faire la connaissance* (*de*) which means to meet, make the acquaintance (of).

Enchanté *de faire votre connaissance*, madame.
I am delighted to meet you, madam.

Valoir (**to be worth**)

Valoir (to be worth) is used in the third person singular in a number of expressions.

Il ne vaut pas la peine d'y aller.
It's not worth while going there.

Il vaudra mieux se taire.
It will be better to keep quiet.

Venir (**to come**)

The present tense of *venir* + *de* and infinitive means " to have just " + past participle.

Nous *venons d'arriver*.   Il *vient de partir*.
We *have just arrived*.   He *has just left*.

Vouloir (**to want, wish**)

Vouloir may translate " to want," " wish," " be willing," and is also used in a number of important expressions.

vouloir dire (to mean)

Que veut dire ce mot?	Que voulez-vous dire?
What does this word mean?	What do you mean?

Voulez-vous (*bien*) and *voudriez-vous* (*bien*) very often are used to express a polite command, and may be used as a substitute for the imperative or command form, as explained on page 36. *Veuillez* plus infinitive may also be so used, but is not so common.

Veuillez fermer les fenêtres s'il commence à pleuvoir.
Please close the windows if it begins to rain.

Telling Time

In French the verb *être* (to be) is used idiomatically in expressions of time.   Study the following examples:

Quelle heure est-il?
[What hour is it?]
What time is it?

Il est trois heures (précises).
[It is three o'clock (exact).]
It is exactly three o'clock.

Il est deux heures cinq.
[It is two hours five.]
It is five (minutes) past two.

Il est cinq heures moins dix.
[It is five hours less ten.]
It is ten (minutes) to five.

Il est quatre heures et demie.
[It is four hours and a half.]
It is half past four.

Il est six heures et quart.
[It is six hours and a quarter.]
It is quarter past six.

Il est six heures moins le quart.
[It is six hours less the quarter.]
It is a quarter to six.

Il est midi.
It is noon.

Il est minuit.
It is midnight.

Some Useful Expressions

Here are some useful idiomatic expressions which have not appeared in the main body of this little grammar, and which are often neglected by phrase books.

Quelle est la date?	What is the date?
C'est aujourd'hui le premier août (le deux août).	Today is August 1 (August 2).
De rien. Il n'y a pas de quoi. Je vous en prie. }	You are welcome.
à l'américaine	in the American fashion
à la française	in the French fashion
à la fois en même temps }	at the same time
à peu pres	about, approximately
À quoi bon?	What's the use?
au lieu de	instead of
c'est-à-dire	that is to say
d'abord	at first
d'ordinaire	usually, generally
en effet	as a matter of fact
en tout cas	at any rate
encore une fois	once more
entendu	all right, fine, O.K.
bien entendu	of course
N'importe.	It doesn't matter.
par exemple	for example
par ici	this way, through here

par là	that way, through there
pas du tout	not at all
quant à (lui)	as for (him)
sans doute	without doubt, no doubt
Service compris?	Is the tip included?
de temps en temps	from time to time
tout à coup	suddenly
tout à fait	completely, entirely
tout à l'heure	a little while ago, in a little while
tout droit	straight ahead
tout le monde	everybody
toute la semaine	the whole week, all week
toutes les semaines	every week
tout de même ⎫ quand même ⎭	all the same, anyway

Vocabulary Tips

Many words in English and French are exactly the same in both languages. Many others have only minor changes in spelling, and are easily recognized. Study the following vocabulary hints and word lists. They will help you increase your vocabulary by many hundreds of words.

Adjectives

The suffixes *-able, -ible, -al, -ant, -ent* are usually the same in both languages.

admirable	horrible	commercial
confortable	possible	municipal
considérable	terrible	royal

brillant	évident
ignorant	excellent
important	innocent

Study the following French suffixes and their usual English equivalents: *-eux* (*-euse*) = -ous; *-eur* = -or; *-el* = -al; *-ique* = -ic.

dangereux	extérieur	habituel	fanatique
fameux	intérieur	mortel	fantastique
furieux	supérieur	naturel	stratégique

Nouns

The following suffixes are generally the same in French and English: *-ion, -tion, -age, -ice, -ent, -ence.*

* For an extensive list of cognates see section following p. 95.

attention	distraction	courage
fonction	million	passage
opinion	question	village
caprice	accident	différence
justice	instrument	patience
service	moment	silence

Study the following French suffixes and their usual English equivalents: *-eur* = -or, -er; *-té* = -ty; *-ie* = -y; *-ique* = -ic; *-re* = -er.

inspecteur	curiosité	compagnie
porteur	difficulté	énergie
visiteur	qualité	industrie

logique	lettre
musique	membre
république	théâtre

Verbs

As mentioned on page 30, the great majority of all French verbs belong to the 1st conjugation (*-er*). Notice how we may derive the meaning of many of these verbs by observing the following changes in the ending:

1. The *-er* ending drops in English.
   aider   consulter   insister   passer   profiter
2. The French *-er* becomes *-e*.
   arriver   décider   désirer   préparer   refuser
3. The French *-er* becomes *-ate*.
   communiquer   hésiter   indiquer   séparer

False Cognates

Now that we have called attention to the many similarities in French-English vocabulary, we must also point out that there are many pitfalls in words that look and sound alike. Sometimes these words mean entirely different things, other times the French word has other meanings more important than its exact English equivalent. Some of the most common of these *faux amis* (false friends) are given below.

French	*Eng. meaning*
actuel	present (*les conditions actuelles*, present conditions)
actuellement	at the present time
addition	bill or check in a restaurant, as well as addition
assister à	to attend, be present at
attendre	to wait (for)
blesser	to wound
chance	(good) luck or fortune (*Bonne chance!* Good luck!; *Vous avez de la chance*, You are lucky)
client	customer as well as client
commander	to order at a restaurant or in business, as well as to command
correspondance	connection, transfer place; for example, in the Paris subway (*métro*)
dame	lady
défendre	to forbid, prohibit, as well as to defend. A number of public signs begin with *Défense de* . . . (*Défense de fumer*, No smoking)
demander	to ask (for)
déranger	usually to disturb, upset
embrasser	to kiss, as well as to embrace
enchanté	delighted, pleased, as well as enchanted
enfant	child
figure	face
formidable	wonderful, marvelous
friction	massage, rubdown, as well as friction
front	forehead as well as front
glace	ice, ice cream, mirror
histoire	story as well as history
intoxication	(food) poisoning
large	wide, broad

lecture	reading
librairie	bookstore
magasin	shop, store
monnaie	change, small cash
nature	nature, but note these expressions: *nature morte,* still life; *omelette nature,* plain omelet
note	hotel bill, school grade, as well as note, memo
parent	relative as well as parent
patron	usually boss, owner
pension	boarding-house, room and board, as well as pension
phrase	sentence
pièce	room, or play, drama
place	usually seat, job, plaza
prune	plum
regarder	to look at
remarquer	usually to notice
rester	to remain
robe	dress
rose	as an adjective, usually pink; as a noun, rose
société	society, but in commercial language has the sense of company
sympathique	nice, likable, pleasant, applied to persons
tarif	rates, scale of charges, as well as tariff
tour	tour, excursion, and turn (*C'est mon tour,* It's my turn), when masculine. As a feminine noun, tower (*la Tour Eiffel*).
type	type, but also a colloquial term for fellow, guy, character
wagon	railroad car (*wagon-lit,* sleeping car; *wagon-restaurant,* diner)

Vocabulary Building with Cognates

When you study a foreign language, building a vocabulary is often one of the most difficult and laborious tasks. It can mean a great deal of tedious memorization and time-consuming study. Yet an English-speaker is in a fortunate position for learning foreign vocabulary, and his work can be considerably lightened. English is composite in origin, and in its word-trove are to be found thousands of forms that are borrowed from other languages. If you have already studied a foreign language, you probably remember the pleasure you felt when you came upon a word that was like its English counterpart; it immediately became easy to remember and use, since it was linked to something familiar, and it probably stayed in your memory longer than other words.

This word list is based upon a useful principle that until the present has not been widely used—the seeking out of vocabulary resemblances and making full use of them. It would seem to be obvious that the easiest way to obtain a French vocabulary would be to study words that English shares with French. Yet, surprisingly enough, until this present list, there has been no systematic compilation of the words that form the common ground between English and French.

This list contains more than twenty-five hundred French words, together with an equal number of English words that have the same meaning, and are either identical or very close in spelling to the French. Most of these English words have been borrowed from the French, in a long history of borrowings ranging from the Norman Conquest of England to the present day. A few, however, have come from Latin, or Italian, or one of the other Romance languages, and have parallel forms in modern French. Altogether, English shares an enormous part of its vocabulary with French. Estimates vary, but it is safe to say that well over half of the basic working vocabulary of English is represented by parallel forms in French.

The twenty-five hundred words in this list are the most frequently used words that English and French have in common parallel forms. They are all important words in French, all appearing among the top six thousand words in word-frequency counts. This list has been based upon a study of comparative cognates among English, French, and Spanish, submitted by William E. Johnson, Jr. as a master's thesis to the George Peabody School for Teachers. The editors of Dover Publications have collated it with Helen S. Eaton's *Semantic Frequency List* (published by Dover in 1961 as *An English-French-German-Spanish Word Frequency Dictionary*) and have enlarged it accordingly. While this list does not con-

95

tain all the most common words in French (since there are many French words that do not have parallel English forms, especially in situations where we use forms derived from Anglo-Saxon), it will give you many of the words that you are likely to need, and will enable you to express your needs in the easiest way.

Do not go beyond the words in this list, however, in assuming that English and French words that look alike have the same meaning. There are many false analogies between the two languages, and it is not always safe to guess at French words because of their appearance. Many words which were once related in the past have since drifted apart in meaning, and in many other words there are simply chance resemblances between English and French. The French word *chair*, for example, does not mean chair, but flesh or meat; the comparable French form to chair is *chaise*.

If you concentrate on the words of this listing, you will find that you will be able to comprehend a good deal of French, and will be able to express your thoughts with a minimum of memorization. Learn to recast your thoughts in these words when you speak. Instead of thinking (in English) of big and great, think of grand which is close to French *grand*; instead of thinking of let, think of permit. Each of these words has its near equivalent in French, and you will be able to express yourself without ambiguities or misstatements.

Use whatever methods come easiest to you for learning these words. Some language experts advise you simply to read through the list two or three times a day for several weeks, and then to let your mind pick up words unconsciously. The association between English and French in this list is so close, that simply reading and rereading the list will enlarge your vocabulary by hundreds of useful words. Some teachers recommend that you memorize a certain number of words each day, perhaps making sentences with them. There are not many short cuts to learning and study, and this list is one of the few that are of value. Do not be afraid of making mistakes. You may be unidiomatic at times; you may be grammatically incorrect occasionally, but you will probably be understood.

Table of Common Equivalents

There are often slight differences in spelling between French words and their English parallels. On occasion these minor differences may disguise what is basically a common structure. For example, *école* and school, *étude* and study, at first glance have little to do with one another. But if you remember that initial é in French, in some circumstances, is equivalent to initial s in English, you will see the relationships.

The following table indicates some of the more frequent equivalences between English and French. Do not follow it blindly, however, for these spelling differences are by no means universal. Use it simply for suggestions.

French	*English*	*Examples*	
é-	s-	école	school
-re or -ier	-er	rendre	render
-ie, or -e	-y	partie	party
-que	-c	aristocratique	aristocratic
-aine	-en, -an, -any	douzaine	dozen
-eur	-or	acteur	actor
-eux, -euse	-ous	anxieux	anxious
-if	-ive	motif	motive
-ence	-ence	divergence	divergence
-é, -ée	-ed	équipé	equipped

The French suffix -*ment* corresponds to the English adverbial ending -ly.

abandon (v.)	abandonner	accusation	accusation
abbey	abbaye	accused	accusé
abdicate	abdiquer	accustom	accoutumer
aberration	aberration	acid	acide
abject	abject	acquire	acquérir
abnormal	anormal	acquisition	acquisition
aboard	à bord	act (n.)	acte
abolish	abolir	action	action
abolition	abolition	active	actif
abominable	abominable	actor	acteur
abound	abonder	actress	actrice
abrupt	abrupte	adapt	adapter
absence	absence	addition	addition
absent (adj.)	absent	address (n.)	adresse
absent (v.)	absenter (s')	address (v.)	adresser
absolute	absolu	adherent	adhérent
absolutely	absolument	adjourn	adjourner
absorb	absorber	adjudge	adjurer
abstain	abstenir (s')	adjustment	ajustement
abstraction	abstraction	administrate	administrer
absurd	absurde	administration	administration
abundance	abondance	administrative	administratif
abundant	abondant	administrator	administrateur
abuse (n.)	abus	admirable	admirable
abuse (v.)	abuser	admiral	amiral
accelerate	accélérer	admire	admirer
accent (n.)	accent	admission	admission
accentuate	accentuer	admit	admettre
accept	accepter	adolescent (adj.)	adolescent
acceptance	acceptation	adopt	adopter
access	accès	adoption	adoption
accessory	accessoire	adoration	adoration
accident	accident	adore	adorer
acclaim (v.)	acclamer	adroit	adroit
accompany	accompagner	advance (n.)	avance
accomplish	accomplir	advance (v.)	avancer
accomplished	accompli	advantageous	avantageux
accord (n.)	accord	adventure (n.)	aventure
accord (v.)	accorder	adventurer	aventurier
accumulate	accumuler	adversary	adversaire

adversity	adversité	amiability	amabilité
aesthetic	ésthétique	amiable	aimable
affect (v.)	affecter	amicable	amical
affection	affection	amplify	amplifier
affirm	affirmer	amuse	amuser
affirmation	affirmation	amusement	amusement
age	âge	amusing	amusant
aged	âgé	analogous	analogue
agency	agence	analogy	analogie
agent	agent	analysis	analyse
aggravate	aggraver	analyze	analyser
aggression	agression	anarchy	anarchie
agitation	agitation	ancestor	ancêtre
agony	agonie	ancient (adj.)	ancien
agreeable	agréable	anecdote	anecdote
agricultural	agricole	angel	ange
agriculture	agriculture	angle	angle
ah!	ah!	animal	animal
aid (n.)	aide	animate	animer
aid (v.)	aider	annex (n.)	annexe
air (n.)	air	announce	annoncer
alarm (v.)	alarmer	announcement	annonce
album	album	annual	annuel
alcohol	alcool	anterior	antérieur
alcoholic	alcoolique	antique	antique
alert (adj.)	alerte	antiquity	antiquité
align	aligner	anxiety	anxiété
aliment	aliment	anxious	anxieux
alimentation	alimentation	apartment	appartement
alliance	alliance	apparent	apparent
allusion	allusion	apparition	apparition
ally	allié	appeal (n.)	appel
amass	amasser	appearance	apparence
amateur	amateur	appetite	appétit
ambassador	ambassadeur	applaud	applaudir
amber	ambre	application	application
ambition	ambition	apply	appliquer
ambitious	ambitieux	appreciate	apprécier
ameliorate	améliorer	appreciation	appréciation
amend	amender	apprehension	appréhension

apprentice (n.)	apprenti	assimilate	assimiler
apprenticeship	apprentissage	assistance	assistance
approach (n.)	approche	associate (v.)	associer
approach (v.)	approcher	association	association
approbation	approbation	assume	assumer
approve	approuver	assurance	assurance
aptitude	aptitude	assure	assurer
arbitrator	arbitre	assured	assuré
arcade	arcade	assuredly	assurément
architect	architecte	athlete	athlète
architecture	architecture	atmosphere	atmosphère
ardor	ardeur	atom	atome
argument	argument	atrocious	atroce
arid	aride	atrocity	atrocité
aristocracy	aristocratie	attach	attacher
aristocratic	aristocratique	attack (n.)	attaque
arm (v.)	armer	attack (v.)	attaquer
army	armée	attention	attention
arrange	arranger	attentive	attentif
arrangement	arrangement	attentively	attentivement
arrest (n.)	arrêt	attenuate	atténuer
arrival	arrivée	attest	attester
arrive	arriver	attitude	attitude
art	art	attraction	attraction
article	article	attribute (n.)	attribut
articulate	articuler	attribute (v.)	attribuer
artificial	artificiel	audacious	audacieux
artillery	artillerie	auditor	auditeur
artist	artiste	augment	augmenter
artistic	artistique	augmentation	augmentation
ascension	ascension	aurora	aurore
aspect	aspect	austere	austère
aspiration	aspiration	authentic	authentique
assail	assaillir	author	auteur
assassin	assassin	authority	autorité
assassinate	assassiner	authorization	autorisation
assault (n.)	assaut	authorize	autoriser
assemble	assembler	automaton	automate
assembly	assemblée	automobile	automobile
assiduity	assiduité	autumn	automne

auxiliary	auxiliaire	benediction	bénédiction
avenue	avenue	benefice	bénéfice
aversion	aversion	Bible	Bible
avid	avide	bile	bile
avidity	avidité	bizarre	bizarre
azure	azur	blame (v.)	blâmer
		blasphemy	blasphème
baby	bébé	block (n.)	bloc
baggage	bagage	blond	blond
bah!	bah!	blouse	blouse
balance (n.)	balance	bomb (n.)	bombe
balance (v.)	balancer	boulevard	boulevard
balcony	balcon	bound (v.)	bondir
ball (party)	bal	bourgeois	bourgeois
ball	balle	boxer	boxeur
ballad	ballade	bracelet	bracelet
balloon	ballon	branch (n.)	branche
banal	banal	brave	brave
banana	banane	bravery	bravoure
band	bande	bravo	bravo
bandit	bandit	brick	brique
bank (n.)	banque	brief	bref
banker	banquier	brigade	brigade
banquet	banquet	brigand	brigand
baptism	baptême	brilliant	brillant
baptize	baptiser	bronze	bronze
bar (n.)	barre	brusque	brusque
bar (v.)	barrer	brutal	brutal
barbarian	barbare	brute	brute
barbarity	barbarie	budget	budget
bark	barque	bureau	bureau
baron	baron	burlesque	burlesque
barrier	barrière	bust (n.)	buste
base (n.)	base	butchery	boucherie
battalion	bataillon	butt (v.)	buter
baton	bâton	button	bouton
battery	batterie		
battle (n.)	bataille	cabin	cabine
bayonet	baïonnette	cable	câble
beauty	beauté	cabriolet	cabriolet

cadaver	cadavre	cause (*n.*)	cause
cafe	café	cavalier	cavalier
cage	cage	cavalry	cavalerie
calculate	calculer	cede	céder
calendar	calendrier	celebrate	célébrer
calm (*adj.*)	calme	celestial	céleste
calm (*v.*)	calmer	cell	cellule
calumny	calomnie	cement (*n.*)	cément
calvary	calvaire	cemetery	cimetière
camp (*n.*)	camp	center (*n.*)	centre
camp (*v.*)	camper	centimeter	centimètre
canal	canal	central	central
canape	canapé	ceremony	cérémonie
candid	candide	certainly	certainement
candidate	candidat	certitude	certitude
candor	candeur	chagrin	chagrin
canon	canon	chamber	chambre
canton	canton	champagne	champagne
capable	capable	champion	champion
capacity	capacité	chance (*n.*)	chance
capital (*adj.*)	capital	change (*v.*)	changer
capital (*n.*)	capitale	chant (*n.*)	chant
caprice	caprice	chant (*v.*)	chanter
capricious	capricieux	chaos	chaos
captain	capitaine	chapel	chapelle
captivate	captiver	chaplet	chapelet
caravan	caravane	chapter	chapitre
cardinal	cardinal	character	caractère
caress (*n.*)	caresse	characteristic	caractéristique
caress (*v.*)	caresser	characterize	caractériser
carpenter	charpentier	charge (*n.*)	charge
carton	carton	charge (*v.*)	charger
cascade	cascade	charity	charité
case	cas	charm (*n.*)	charme
casserole	casserole	charm (*v.*)	charmer
caste	caste	charming	charmant
catastrophe	catastrophe	chase (*v.*)	chasser
category	catégorie	chaste	chaste
cathedral	cathédrale	chateau	château
catholic	catholique	chauffeur	chauffeur

chemise	chemise	collection	collection
chevalier	chevalier	collective	collectif
chic	chic	collectivity	collectivité
chief	chef	colonel	colonel
chocolate	chocolat	colonial	coloniale
choice	choix	colony	colonie
cigar	cigare	color (n.)	couleur
cigarette	cigarette	color (v.)	colorer
circle	cercle	colored	coloré
circuit	circuit	colossal	colossal
circular (adj.)	circulaire	colossus	colosse
circulate	circuler	combat (n.)	combat
circulation	circulation	combat (v.)	combattre
circumstance	circonstance	combination	combinaison
circus	cirque	combine	combiner
citadel	citadelle	comedian	comédien
citation	citation	comedy	comédie
cite	citer	comet	comète
civil	civil	comfortable	confortable
civilization	civilisation	comfortably	confortablement
civilize	civiliser	comical	comique
clamor (n.)	clameur	commandant	commandant
class (n.)	classe	commandment	commandement
class (v.)	classer	commence	commencer
classic	classique	commencement	commencement
clef	clef	commerce	commerce
clement	clément	commercial	commercial
clergy	clergé	commissary	commissaire
client	client	commission	commission
clientele	clientèle	commissioner	commissionnaire
climate	climat	commit	commettre
closed	clos	commodious	commode
club	club	common	commun
cock	coq	communicate	communiquer
code	code	communication	communication
cohesion	cohésion	communion	communion
coincidence	coïncidence	companion	compagnon
collaboration	collaboration	comparable	comparable
collaborator	collaborateur	compare	comparer
colleague	collègue	comparison	comparaison

compatriot	compatriote
compensation	compensation
complement	complément
complete (adj.)	complet
complete (v.)	compléter
complex	complexe
complicate	compliquer
complicated	compliqué
complication	complication
complicity	complicité
compliment	compliment
comport (v.)	comporter
compose	composer
composition	composition
comprehend	comprendre
compromise (n.)	compromis
concede	concéder
conceive	concevoir
concentrate	concentrer
concentration	concentration
conception	conception
concern (v.)	concerner
concert	concert
concession	concession
conciliate	concilier
conciliation	conciliation
conclude	conclure
concourse	concours
concurrence	concurrence
condemn	condamner
condemnation	condamnation
condense	condenser
condition	condition
conductor	conducteur
cone	cône
confer	conférer
conference	conférence
confess	confesser
confession	confession
confidence	confidence

confident (n.)	confident
confidential	confidentiel
confine (v.)	confiner
confirm	confirmer
conflict (n.)	conflit
confrere	confrère
confusion	confusion
congress	congrès
conjure	conjurer
conquer	conquérir
conquest	conquête
conscience	conscience
consent (n.)	consentement
consent (v.)	consentir
consequence	conséquence
conserve	conserver
consider	considérer
considerable	considérable
consideration	considération
consist	consister
consolation	consolation
console	consoler
conspirator	conspirateur
constant	constant
constitute	constituer
constitution	constitution
constraint	contrainte
consul	consul
consult	consulter
consume	consommer
consummation	consommation
contact (n.)	contact
contagious	contagieux
contain	contenir
contemplation	contemplation
contemporary	contemporain
content (adj.)	content
continent (adj.)	continent
continual	continuel
continue	continuer

contour	contour	courageously	courageusement
contract (*v.*)	contracter	courtesy	courtoisie
contradict	contredire	cousin	cousin
contradiction	contradiction	cover (*n.*)	couvert
contrarily	contrairement	cover (*v.*)	couvrir
contrary	contraire	crab	crabe
contrast (*n.*)	contraste	crack (*v.*)	craquer
contrast (*v.*)	contraster	cravat	cravate
contribute	contribuer	cream	crème
contribution	contribution	creation	création
convention	convention	creator	créateur
conversation	conversation	creature	créature
converse (*v.*)	converser	credit (*n.*)	crédit
conversion	conversion	crepe	crêpe
convert (*v.*)	convertir	crepuscule	crépuscule
conviction	conviction	crime	crime
convoke	convoquer	criminal	criminel
convoy	convoi	crisis	crise
copy (*n.*)	copie	critic	critique
copy (*v.*)	copier	criticism	critique
cord	corde	cruel	cruel
cordial	cordial	cry (*n.*)	cri
corporation	corporation	cry (*v.*)	crier
correct (*adj.*)	correct	crystal	cristal
correction	correction	cube	cube
correctly	correctement	cultivate	cultiver
correspond	correspondre	cultivator	cultivateur
correspondence	correspondance	culture	culture
correspondent	correspondant	cure (*n.*)	cure
corridor	corridor	curiosity	curiosité
corruption	corruption	curious	curieux
cortege	cortège		
costume	costume	damage	dommage
cotton	coton	dame	dame
countenance	contenance	damn	damner
countess	comtesse	dance (*n.*)	danse
couple	couple	dance (*v.*)	danser
couplet	couplet	danger	danger
courage	courage	dangerous	dangereux
courageous	courageux	date (*n.*)	date

date (*v.*)	dater	deliver	délivrer
debate	débat	deliverance	délivrance
debris	débris	deluge (*n.*)	déluge
debtor	débiteur	democracy	démocratie
debut	début	democratic	démocratique
decadence	décadence	demolish	démolir
deceive	décevoir	demonstrate	démontrer
deception	déception	demonstration	démonstration
decide	décider (se)	denounce	dénoncer
decision	décision	dense	dense
decisive	décisif	departure	départ
declaration	déclaration	dependence	dépendance
declare	déclarer	deplorable	déplorable
decline (*n.*)	déclin	deplore	déplorer
decompose	décomposer	deputy	député
decorate	décorer	descend	descendre
decoration	décor	descendant	descendant
	décoration	description	description
deduction	déduction	desert (*n.*)	désert
defeat (*n.*)	défaite	desert (*v.*)	déserter
defective	défectueux	desirable	désirable
defense	défense	desire (*n.*)	désir
defiance	défiance	desire (*v.*)	désirer
defile	défiler	desirous	désireux
define	définir	desolate (*v.*)	désoler
definite	définitif	despair (*n.*)	désespoir
definition	définition	despair (*v.*)	désespérer
defunct	défunt	dessert	dessert
defy	défier	destination	destination
degenerate (*v.*)	dégenerer	destine	destiner
degree	degré	destiny	destin
deign	daigner		destinée
deity	déité	destruction	destruction
delegate (*v.*)	déléguer	detach	détacher
delegation	délégation	detachment	détachement
deliberate (*v.*)	délibérer	detail	détail
delicacy	délicatesse	determine	déterminer
delicate	délicat	detest	détester
delicious	délicieux	detestable	détestable
delirium	délire	detour (*n.*)	détour

detriment	détriment	disguise (v.)	déguiser
devastate	dévaster	dishonor (n.)	déshonneur
develop	développer	disorder (n.)	désordre
development	développement	dispense	dispenser
devour	dévorer	disperse	disperser
devout	dévoué	dispose	disposer
dialogue	dialogue	disposition	disposition
diamond	diamant	dispute (n.)	dispute
dictate	dicter	dispute (v.)	disputer
dictionary	dictionnaire	dissipate	dissiper
difference	différence	distance (n.)	distance
different	différent	distant	distant
difficult	difficile	distinct	distinct
difficulty	difficulté	distinction	distinction
digest (v.)	digérer	distinguish	distinguer
digestion	digestion	distraction	distraction
dignity	dignité	distress (n.)	détresse
dimension	dimension	distribute	distribuer
diminish	diminuer	distribution	distribution
dine (v.)	dîner	divan	divan
dinner (n.)	dîner	divergence	divergence
diocese	diocèse	divert	divertir
diplomatic	diplomatique	divine (adj.)	divin
direct (adj.)	direct	division	division
direction	direction	divorce (v.)	divorcer
director	directeur	docile	docile
disagreeable	désagréable	doctor	docteur
disarm (v.)	désarmer	doctrine	doctrine
disaster	désastre	document	document
disc	disque	dogma	dogme
discern	discerner	domain	domaine
discharge (v.)	décharger	domicile	domicile
disciple	disciple	dominate	dominer
disconcert	déconcerter	domination	domination
discourage	décourager	double (adj.)	double
discourse (n.)	discours	double (v.)	doubler
discreet	discret	doubt (n.)	doute
discretion	discrétion	doubt (v.)	douter
discussion	discussion	dozen	douzaine
disdain (n.)	dédain	dragon	dragon

drama	drame	elite	élite
dramatic	dramatique	eloquence	éloquence
droll	drôle	eloquent	éloquent
duchess	duchesse	emanate	émaner
duel (n.)	duel	embalm	embaumer
dupe (n.)	dupe	embark	embarquer
durable	durable	embassy	ambassade
dynasty	dynastie	embellish	embellir
		emblem	emblème
east	est	embrace (v.)	embrasser
ebullition	ébullition	emerald	émeraude
eccentricity	excentricité	emigration	émigration
ecclesiastical	ecclésiastique	emigre	émigré
echo (n.)	écho	eminent	éminent
economic	économique	emit	émettre
economy	économie	emotion	émotion
edict	édit	emperor	empereur
edifice	édifice	emphasis	emphase
edify	édifier	empire	empire
edition	édition	employ (n.)	emploi
efface	effacer	employ (v.)	employer
effect (n.)	effet	employee	employé
effective	effectif	enchain	enchaîner
effort	effort	enchant	enchanter
effusion	effusion	enchantment	enchantement
egoism	égoïsme	encourage	encourager
egoist	égoïste	enemy	ennemi
elaboration	élaboration	energetic	énergique
election	élection	energy	énergie
elector	électeur	enervate	énerver
electoral	électoral	engage	engager
electric	électrique	engender	engendrer
electricity	électricité	ennoble	ennoblir
elegance	élégance	enormous	énorme
elegant	élégant	enrage	enrager
element	élément	enrich	enrichir
elephant	éléphant	enter	entrer
elevate	élever	enterprise	entreprise
elevation	élévation	enthusiasm	enthousiasme
eliminate	éliminer	enthusiast	enthousiaste

entire	entier	exactly	exactement
entitle	intituler	exaggerate	exagérer
enumerate	énumérer	exaggeration	exagération
envelop (n.)	enveloppe	exalt	exalter
envelop (v.)	envelopper	exaltation	exaltation
envy (n.)	envie	examination	examen
episode	épisode	examine	examiner
epoch	époque	example	exemple
equality	égalité	excel	exceller
equilibrate	équilibrer	excellence	excellence
equilibrium	équilibre	excellent	excellent
equip	équiper	except (prep.)	excepté
equipment	équipment	exception	exception
equity	équité	exceptional	exceptionel
equivalent	équivalent	exceptionally	exceptionellement
era	ère	excess	excès
err (v.)	errer	excessive	excessif
errant	errant	exchange (n.)	échange
error	erreur	exchange (v.)	échanger
essay (n.)	essai	excitation	excitation
essence	essence	excite	exciter
essential	essentiel	exclude	exclure
establish	établir	exclusive	exclusif
establishment	établissement	exclusively	exclusivement
estimable	estimable	excursion	excursion
eternal	éternel	excuse (n.)	excuse
eternally	éternellement	excuse (v.)	excuser
eternity	éternité	execute	exécuter
eternize	éterniser	executor	exécuteur
evacuate	évacuer	execution	exécution
evade	évader	exemption	exemption
evaluate	évaluer	exercise (n.)	exercise
eventual	éventuel	exercise (v.)	exercer
evidence	évidence	exhale	exhaler
evident	évident	exhibition	exhibition
evidently	évidemment	exigency	exigence
evoke	évoquer	exile (n.)	exil
evolution	évolution	exile (v.)	exiler
exact	exact	exist	exister
exactitude	exactitude	existence	existence

exotic	exotique	fanaticism	fanatisme
expansion	expansion	fanfare	fanfare
expedition	expédition	fantastic	fantastique
expel	expulser	farce	farce
experimental	expérimental	fatality	fatalité
expert	expert	fatally	fatalement
expire	expirer	fatigue (n.)	fatigue
explication	explication	fatigue (v.)	fatiguer
exploit (n.)	exploit	favor (n.)	faveur
exploit (v.)	exploiter	favor (v.)	favoriser
exploitation	exploitation	favorable	favorable
exploration	exploration	favorite (n.)	favori
explore	explorer	favorite (adj.)	favori
explosion	explosion	fecund	fécond
exportation	exportation	federation	fédération
expose (v.)	exposer	felicitate	féliciter
exposition	exposition	felicitation	félicitation
expression	expression	felicity	félicité
expressive	expressif	feminine	féminin
exquisite	exquis	ferment (v.)	fermenter
extension	extension	ferocious	féroce
exterior	extérieur	fertile	fertile
extraction	extraction	fervent	fervent
extravagant	extravagant	fervor	ferveur
extreme	extrême	fever	fièvre
extremely	extrêmement	fiance	fiancé
extremity	extrémité	fiber	fibre
		fidelity	fidélité
fable	fable	figure (n.)	figure
fabricate	fabriquer	file (n.) (row)	file
fabrication	fabrication	filial	filial
fabulous	fabuleux	final	final
facade	façade	finally	finalement
facilitate	faciliter	finance (n.)	finance
facility	facilité	financial	financier
faction	faction	finesse	finesse
faculty	faculté	fix (v.)	fixer
family	famille	fixed	fixé
famine	famine	flagrant	flagrant
famous	fameux	flame	flamme

flank (*n.*)	flanc	gaiety	gaieté
flannel	flanelle	gain (*n.*)	gain
flatter	flatter	gallant	galant
fluid	fluide	gallantry	galanterie
folly	folie	gallery	galerie
force (*v.*)	forcer	gallop (*n.*)	galop
forced	forcé	gamin	gamin
forge (*n.*)	forge	garage	garage
form (*n.*)	forme	garden	jardin
form (*v.*)	former	gay	gai
formality	formalité	gendarme	gendarme
formation	formation	general (*adj.*)	général
formidable	formidable	general (*n.*)	général
formula	formule	generality	généralité
formulate	formuler	generalize	généraliser
fortify	fortifier	generally	généralement
fortress	forteresse	generation	génération
fortune	fortune	generosity	générosité
foundation	fondation	generous	généreux
founder	fondateur	genius	génie
fracas	fracas	genteel	gentil
fraction	fraction	geometrical	géométrique
fragile	fragile	geranium	géranium
franchise	franchise	germinate	germer
frank	franc	gesticulate	gesticuler
frequent (*adj.*)	fréquent	gesture	geste
frequent (*v.*)	fréquenter	giant	géant
frivolity	frivolité	gigantic	gigantesque
frontier	frontière	glacial	glacial
fruit	fruit	globe	globe
fugitive (*n.*)	fugitif	glorious	glorieux
function (*n.*)	fonction	glory	gloire
function (*v.*)	fonctionner	golf	golf
functionary	fonctionnaire	gorge (*n.*)	gorge
fundamental	fondamental	gothic	gothique
furious	furieux	gourmand	gourmand
furtive	furtif	gourmet	gourmet
fury	fureur	govern (*v.*)	gouverner
	furie	government	gouvernement
future (*adj.*)	futur	governor	gouverneur

gracious	gracieux	heroic	héroique
grain	grain	heroism	héroisme
grammar	grammaire	hesitate	hésiter
grandeur	grandeur	hesitation	hésitation
grandiose	grandiose	hideous	hideux
gratis	gratuit	historian	historien
gratitude	gratitude	historic	historique
grave (adj.)	grave	homage	hommage
gravity	gravité	homogeneous	homogène
grimace (n.)	grimace	honesty	honnêteté
grotesque	grotesque	honor (n.)	honneur
group (n.)	groupe	honor (v.)	honorer
group (v.)	grouper	honorable	honorable
guarantee (n.)	garantie	horizon	horizon
guardian	gardien	horizontal	horizontal
guide (n.)	guide	horrible	horrible
guide (v.)	guider	horror	horreur
guillotine	guillotine	hospital	hôpital
guise	guise	hospitality	hospitalité
guitar	guitare	hostile	hostile
gymnasium	gymnase	hostility	hostilité
		hotel	hôtel
habit	habitude	human	humain
habitation	habitation	humanity	humanité
habitual	habituel	humble	humble
habitually	habituellement	humbly	humblement
hatchet	hache	humid	humide
haggard	hagard	humidity	humidité
harangue (n.)	harangue	humiliate	humilier
harass	harasser	humiliation	humiliation
hardy	hardi	humility	humilité
harmonious	harmonieux	humor (n.)	humeur
harmony	harmonie	hut	hutte
hazardous	hasardeux	hydrogen	hydrogène
herb	herbe	hygiene	hygiène
hereditary	héréditaire	hymn	hymne
heresy	hérésie	hypocrisy	hypocrisie
heretic	hérétique	hypothesis	hypothèse
heritage	héritage		
hero	héros	idea	idée

ideal	idéal	importunate	importun
identical	identique	impose	imposer
identity	identité	imposing	imposant
idiot	idiot	impossibility	impossibilité
ignoble	ignoble	impossible	impossible
ignorance	ignorance	impression	impression
ignorant	ignorant	imprison	emprisonner
illuminate	illuminer	improvise	improviser
illusion	illusion	imprudence	imprudence
illustrate	illustrer	impudent	impudent
illustration	illustration	impulsion	impulsion
image	image	impure	impur
imaginary	imaginaire	inaugurate	inaugurer
imagination	imagination	incapacity	incapacité
imagine	imaginer (s')	incessant	incessant
imbecile	imbécile	incident	incident
imitate	imiter	inclination	inclination
imitation	imitation	incline (v.)	incliner (s')
immediate	immédiat	incomparable	incomparable
immediately	immédiatement	incompatible	incompatible
immense	immense	incomplete	incomplet
imminent	imminent	incomprehensible	incompréhensible
immobility	immobilité	incontestable	incontestable
immolate	immoler	inconvenient	inconvénient
immortal	immortel	incredible	incroyable
impartial	impartial	indecision	indécision
impassible	impassible	indefinite	indéfini
impatience	impatience	independence	indépendance
impatient	impatient	independent	indépendant
imperceptible	imperceptible	indicate	indiquer
impertinence	impertinence	indication	indication
impetuous	impétueux	indifference	indifférence
implacable	implacable	indifferent	indifférent
implicate	impliquer	indignation	indignation
implore	implorer	indirect	indirect
impolite	impoli	indiscreet	indiscret
import (v.)	importer	indiscretion	indiscrétion
importance	importance	indispensable	indispensable
important	important	individual (n.)	individu
importation	importation	individual (adj.)	individuel

indulgence	indulgence	inspection	inspection
indulgent	indulgent	inspector	inspecteur
industrial	industriel	inspiration	inspiration
industry	industrie	inspire	inspirer
inert	inerte	install	installer
inevitable	inévitable	installation	installation
inexplicable	inexplicable	instance	instance
inextricable	inextricable	instant	instant
infamous	infâme	instinct	instinct
inferior	inférieur	instinctive	instinctif
infinite	infini	institute (n.)	institut
inflict	infliger	institute (v.)	instituer
influence (n.)	influence	institution	institution
influence (v.)	influencer	instruction	instruction
influential	influent	instrument	instrument
inform	informer	insufficiency	insuffisance
ingenious	ingénieux	insufficient	insuffisant
ingratitude	ingratitude	insular	insulaire
inhabit	habiter	insult (n.)	insulte
inhabitant	habitant	insult (v.)	insulter
inherit	hériter	insupportable	insupportable
inheritor	héritier	insurgent	insurgé
initial	initial	intact	intact
initiative	initiative	integral	intégral
injustice	injustice	integrity	intégrité
innocence	innocence	intellectual	intellectuel
innocent	innocent	intelligence	intelligence
inoffensive	inoffensif	intelligent	intelligent
inscribe	inscrire	intendant	intendant
inscription	inscription	intense	intense
insect	insecte	intensity	intensité
insensible	insensible	intention	intention
inseparable	inséparable	inter	enterrer
insignificant	insignifiant	interest (n.)	interêt
insinuate	insinuer	interest (v.)	intéresser
insist	insister	interested (adj.)	intéressé
insistence	insistance	interested (v.)	intéresser (s')
insolence	insolence	interesting	intéressant
insolent	insolent	interior	intérieur
inspect	inspecter	intermediate	intermédiaire

interminable	interminable	irritate	irriter
international	international	irruption	irruption
interpellation	interpellation	isolate	isoler
interpret	interpréter	isolated	isolé
interpretation	interprétation	issue (n.)	issue
interpreter	interprète	ivory	ivoire
interrogate	interroger		
interrupt	interrompre	jealousy	jalousie
interruption	interruption	journal	journal
interval	intervalle	joy	joie
intervene	intervenir	joyous	joyeux
intervention	intervention	judge (n.)	juge
intimacy	intimité	judge (v.)	juger
intimidate	intimider	judgment	jugement
intolerable	intolérable	judiciary	judiciaire
intonation	intonation	judicious	judicieux
intrepid	intrépide	jury	jury
intrigue (v.)	intriguer	just (adj.)	juste
introduce	introduire	justice	justice
introduction	introduction	justify	justifier
intuition	intuition		
inundate	inonder	kilogram	kilogramme
inundation	inondation	kilometer	kilomètre
invasion	invasion		
invent	inventer	laboratory	laboratoire
invention	invention	laic	laïque
inventor	inventeur	lamentable	lamentable
inverse	inverse	lamp	lampe
investigation	investigation	langor	langueur
invincible	invincible	language	langue
invisible	invisible		langage
invite	inviter	lantern	lanterne
invoke	invoquer	lassitude	lassitude
involuntary	involontaire	laurel	laurier
ironic	ironique	league	ligue
irony	ironie	legal	légal
irreparable	irréparable	legend	légende
irreproachable	irréprochable	legion	légion
irresistible	irrésistible	legislator	législateur
irresolute	irrésolu	legitimate	légitime

legume	légume	malefactor	malfaiteur
lemonade	limonade	malice	malice
letter	lettre	mamma	maman
lettered	lettré	maneuver (*n.*)	manoeuvre
liberal	libéral	maneuver (*v.*)	manoeuvrer
liberate	libérer	manifest (*adj.*)	manifeste
liberty	liberté	manifest (*v.*)	manifester
lieutenant	lieutenant	manifestation	manifestation
limit (*n.*)	limite	manual (*adj.*)	manuel
limit (*v.*)	limiter	manuscript	manuscrit
limpid	limpide	march (*n.*)	marche
lion	lion	march (*v.*)	marcher
liquid	liquide	marine (*adj.*)	marin
liquidate	liquider	marine (*n.*)	marine
liquor	liqueur	maritime	maritime
literature	littérature	mark (*n.*)	marque
livid	livide	marriage	mariage
locality	localité	marry	marier
locomotive	locomotive	marshal	maréchal
lodge (*v.*)	loger	martyr (*n.*)	martyr
loge	loge	marvel (*n.*)	merveille
logical	logique	mask (*n.*)	masque
long (*adj.*)	long	mask (*v.*)	masquer
loyal	loyal	mass (*n.*)	masse
loyalty	loyauté	massacre (*n.*)	massacre
lucid	lucide	massacre (*v.*)	massacrer
lugubrious	lugubre	massive	massif
luminous	lumineux	match (*n.*) (sports)	match
lyrical	lyrique	material (*adj.*)	matériel
		materials	matériaux
magic	magique	maternal	maternel
magistrate	magistrat	mathematical	mathématique
magnificent	magnifique	maturity	maturité
maintain	maintenir	maximum	maximum
majestic	majestueux	measure (*n.*)	mesure
majesty	majesté	measure (*v.*)	mesurer
major (*adj.*)	majeur	mechanical	mécanique
majority	majorité	mechanism	mécanisme
malady	maladie	medal	médaille
male	mâle	medical	médical

medicine	médicine	miserable	misérable
mediocre	médiocre	misery	misère
mediocrity	médiocrité	mission	mission
meditate	méditer	mobile	mobile
meditation	méditation	mobility	mobilité
melancholic	mélancolique	mobilize	mobiliser
melancholy	mélancolie	mockery	moquerie
member	membre	mode	mode
memorable	mémorable	model (n.)	modèle
memory	mémoire	model (v.)	modeler
menace (n.)	menace	moderate (v.)	modérer
menace (v.)	menacer	moderation	modération
mental	mental	modern	moderne
mention (v.)	mentionner	modest	modeste
menu	menu	modesty	modestie
merchandise	marchandise	modification	modification
meridional	méridional	modify	modifier
merit (n.)	mérite	moment (n.)	moment
merit (v.)	mériter	monarch	monarque
metal	métal	monastery	monastère
metallic	métallique	monopoly	monopole
meter	mètre	monotonous	monotone
method	méthode	monotony	monotonie
methodic	méthodique	monster	monstre
metropolis	métropole	monstrous	monstrueux
migraine	migraine	monument	monument
military	militaire	monumental	monumental
million	million	moral (adj.)	moral
mine (n.)	mine	moral (n.)	morale
miner	mineur	moralist	moraliste
miniature	miniature	morality	moralité
minimum	minimum	mortal	mortel
ministry	ministère	motive	motif
minor (n.)	mineur	motor	moteur
minority	minorité	mount (n.)	mont
minute (adj.)	minutieux	move (v.)	mouvoir
minute (n.)	minute	movement	mouvement
miracle	miracle	mule	mule
miraculous	miraculeux	multiply	multiplier
mirror (n.)	miroir	multitude	multitude

municipal	municipal	nervous	nerveux
municipality	municipalité	niece	nièce
murmur (*n.*)	murmure	no	non
murmur (*v.*)	murmurer	noble	noble
muscle	muscle	nobly	noblement
muse (*n.*)	muse	nocturnal	nocturne
museum	musée	nomination	nomination
music	musique	normal	normal
musician	musicien	notable	notable
muslin	mousseline	note (*n.*)	note
Mussulman	musulman	note (*v.*)	noter
mustache	moustache	notion	notion
mute	muet	nourish	nourrir
mutilate	mutiler	nuance	nuance
mutton	mouton	nullity	nullité
mysterious	mystérieux	number	numéro
mystery	mystère	nymph	nymphe
mystic (*adj.*)	mystique		
mystification	mystification	obey	obéir
		object (*n.*)	objet
naive	naïf	object (*v.*)	objecter
naivete	naïveté	objection	objection
natal	natal	objective	objectif
nation	nation	obligation	obligation
national	national	obligatory	obligatoire
nationality	nationalité	oblige	obliger
natural	naturel	oblique	oblique
naturally	naturellement	obscure (*adj.*)	obscur
nature	nature	obscurity	obscurité
naval	naval	observation	observation
navigation	navigation	observe	observer
necessarily	nécessairement	observer	observateur
necessary	nécessaire	obstacle	obstacle
necessitate	nécessiter	obstruct	obstruer
necessity	nécessité	obtain	obtenir
negative	négatif	occasion	occasion
neglect (*v.*)	négliger	occidental	occidental
negligence	négligence	occupation	occupation
negligent	négligent	occupy	occuper
Negro	nègre	ocean	océan

odious	odieux
odor	odeur
offend	offenser
offer (n.)	offre
offer (v.)	offrir
officer	officier
officially	officiellement
omnibus	omnibus
onion	oignon
opera	opéra
operate	opérer
operation	opération
opinion	opinion
oppose	opposer
opposite	oppose
opposition	opposition
oppression	oppression
optimism	optimisme
optimist	optimiste
orator	orateur
orchestra	orchestre
order (n.)	ordre
ordinance	ordonnance
ordinarily	ordinairement
ordinary	ordinaire
organic	organique
organism	organisme
organization	organisation
organize	organiser
Orient	orient
oriental	oriental
orifice	orifice
origin	origine
original	original
originality	originalité
ornament	ornement
orphan	orphelin
orthography	orthographe
oscillate	osciller
overture	ouverture

pacific	pacifique
pact	pacte
page (n.)	page
palace	palais
pale (adj.)	pâle
panic	panique
papa	papa
parade (n.)	parade
paradise	paradis
paragraph	paragraphe
parallel	parallèle
paralyze	paralyser
pardon (n.)	pardon
pardon (v.)	pardonner
parent	parent
parliament	parlement
parliamentary	parlementaire
part (n.)	part
participate	participer
participation	participation
particular	particulier
partner	partenaire
party (pol.)	partie
pass (v.)	passer
passage	passage
passion	passion
passionate	passionné
passionately	passionnément
pastor	pasteur
paternal	paternel
pathetic	pathétique
patience	patience
patient (adj.)	patient
patriot	patriote
patriotism	patriotisme
patron	patron
patronage	patronage
pave (v.)	paver
pavilion	pavillon
pay (v.)	payer

payment	paiement	pest	peste
peach	pêche	petroleum	pétrole
pearl	perle	phantom	fantôme
pedant	pédant	pharmacist	pharmacien
pell-mell	pêle-mêle	pharmacy	pharmacie
penchant	penchant	phase	phase
pendulum	pendule	phenomena	phénomène
penetrate	pénétrer	philosopher	philosophe
pension (n.)	pension	philosophy	philosophie
pensive	pensif	phosphorus	phosphore
penumbra	pénombre	photograph (n.)	photographie
people	peuple	photograph (v.)	photographier
perceive	percevoir	phrase	phrase
perceptible	perceptible	physical	physique
perch (v.)	percher	physiognomy	physionomie
perfect (v.)	perfectionner	piano	piano
perfection	perfection	pick (n.)	pic
perfidious	perfide	picturesque	pittoresque
perfume (n.)	parfum	piece	pièce
perfume (v.)	parfumer	piety	piété
peril	péril	pigeon	pigeon
perilous	périlleux	pillage (n.)	pillage
period	période	pilot (n.)	pilote
periodic	périodique	pipe (n.)	pipe
perish	périr	pirate	pirate
permission	permission	pistol	pistolet
permit (n.)	permis	pity	pitié
permit (v.)	permettre	place (n.)	place
perpetual	perpétuel	place (v.)	placer
persecute	persécuter	plain (n.)	plaine
persecution	persécution	plan (n.)	plan
persevere	persévérer	planet	planète
persist	persister	plant (n.)	plante
person	personne	plant (v.)	planter
personal	personnel	plateau	plateau
personality	personnalité	pleasantry	plaisanterie
personally	personnellement	plunge (v.)	plonger
perspective	perspective	poem	poème
perspicacious	perspicace	poet	poète
persuade	persuader	poetical	poétique

poetry	poésie	precipitation	précipitation
point (n.) (place)	point	precise	précis
point (n.)	pointe	precisely	précisement
poison (n.)	poison	precision	précision
polar	polaire	predict	prédire
polemic	polémique	predominance	prédominance
police	police	prefect	préfet
politeness	politesse	prefecture	préfecture
political	politique	prefer	préférer
pomp	pompe	preferable	préférable
popular	populaire	preference	préférence
population	population	prelate	prélat
porcelain	porcelaine	preliminary	préliminaire
pork	porc	preoccupation	préoccupation
port	port	preoccupied	préoccupé
portfolio	portefeuille	preparation	préparation
portion	portion	prepare	préparer
portrait	portrait	prerogative	prérogative
position	position	presence	présence
positive	positif	present (adj.)	présent
possession	possession	present (adv.)	présent
possessor	possesseur	present (v.)	présenter
possibility	possibilité	presentation	présentation
possible	possible	presentiment	présentiment
post	poste	preside	présider
postal	postal	presidency	présidence
pot	pot	president	président
poverty	pauvreté	press (n.)	presse
powder	poudre	press (v.)	presser
practical	pratique	pressed	pressé
practice (n.)	pratique	prestige	prestige
practice (v.)	pratiquer	presume	présumer
preach	prêcher	pretend	prétendre
precaution	précaution	pretention	prétention
precede	précéder	pretext	prétexte
precedent	précédent	prevision	prévision
precept	précepte	primitive	primitif
precious	précieux	princess	princesse
precipice	précipice	principal	principal
precipitate	précipiter	principally	principalement

principle (n.)	principe	proprietor	propriétaire
prism	prisme	prose	prose
prison	prison	prosperity	prospérité
prisoner	prisonnier	prosperous	prospère
privation	privation	protection	protection
privilege	privilège	protector	protecteur
probable	probable	protest (v.)	protester
problem	problème	protestant	protestant
proceed (v.)	procéder	protestantism	protestantisme
procession	procession	protestation	protestation
proclaim	proclamer	prove	prouver
proclamation	proclamation	proverb	proverbe
procure	procurer	providence	providence
prodigious	prodigieux	province	province
produce (v.)	produire	provincial	provincial
producer	producteur	provision	provision
product	produit	prudence	prudence
production	production	prudent	prudent
profane (adj.)	profane	public (n.)	public
profession	profession	publication	publication
professor	professeur	publicity	publicité
profile	profil	punish	punir
profit (n.)	profit	pure	pur
profit (v.)	profiter	purely	purement
profoundly	profondément	purify	purifier
program	programme	purity	pureté
progress (n.)	progrès	pyramid	pyramide
progressive	progressif		
project (n.)	projet	qualify	qualifier
prolong	prolonger	quality	qualité
promenade	promenade	quantity	quantité
promise (n.)	promesse	quarrel (n.)	querelle
prompt	prompt	quart	quart
promptitude	promptitude	quarter (place)	quartier
pronounce	prononcer	question (n.)	question
propaganda	propagande	question (v.)	questionner
prophet	prophète	quit	quitter
proportion	proportion		
propose	proposer	race (n.)	race
proposition	proposition	radical	radical

rage (n.)	rage	reform (n.)	réforme
rail (n.)	rail	reform (v.)	réformer
rampart	rempart	refrain (n.)	refrain
rapid	rapide	refuge	refuge
rapidity	rapidité	refuse (v.)	refuser
rare	rare	regard (n.)	regard
rarely	rarement	regime	régime
rat	rat	regiment	régiment
ravage (n.)	ravage	region	région
ravage (v.)	ravager	register (n.)	régistre
reaction	réaction	regret (n.)	regret
reality	réalité	regret (v.)	regretter
reason (n.)	raison	regrettable	regrettable
reason (v.)	raisonner	regular	régulier
reassemble	rassembler	regularity	régularité
reassure	rassurer	regularly	régulièrement
rebel (n.)	rebelle	regulator	régulateur
receive	recevoir	reign (n.)	règne
recent	récent	reimburse	rembourser
reception	réception	relation	relation
recite	réciter	relative (adj.)	relatif
recommence	recommencer	relic	rélique
recommend	recommander	relief	relief
recompense (n.)	récompense	religion	religion
recompense (v.)	récompenser	religious	religieux
reconcile	réconcilier	remark (n.)	remarque
reconstitute	reconstituer	remarkable	remarquable
reconstruct	reconstruire	remedy (n.)	remède
recourse	recours	remedy (v.)	remédier
recreation	récréation	remorse	remords
recruit (v.)	recruter	renaissance	renaissance
rectify	rectifier	render	rendre
redouble (v.)	redoubler	renounce	renoncer
redoubtable	redoutable	repair	réparer
redress (v.)	redresser	reparation	réparation
reduction	réduction	repeat	répéter
refectory	réfectoire	repent	repentir (se)
refined	raffiné	represent	représenter
reflect	refléter	representation	représentation
reflection	réflexion	repression	répression

reprise	reprise	revelation	révélation
reproach (n.)	reproche	revenue	revenu
reproduce	reproduire	reverence	révérence
republic	république	reverie	rêverie
republican	républicain	review	revue
repugnance	répugnance	revolt (n.)	révolte
require	requérir	revolt (v.)	révolter
resemblance	ressemblance	revolutionary	révolutionnaire
resemble	ressembler	rheumatism	rhumatisme
resentment	ressentiment	rhythm	rythme
reserve (n.)	réserve	rich	riche
reserve (v.)	réserver	richness	richesse
reservoir	réservoir	ridiculous	ridicule
reside	résider	rigor	rigueur
residence	résidence	rigorous	rigoureux
resign	résigner	risk (v.)	risquer
resin	résine	rite	rite
resist	résister	rival (n.)	rival
resistance	résistance	robust	robuste
resolution	résolution	rock (n.)	roc
resource	ressource	role	rôle
respect (n.)	respect	romantic	romantique
respect (v.)	respecter	rose	rose
respectable	respectable	rouge	rouge
respective	respectif	round (adj.)	rond
respiration	respiration	route	route
response	réponse	routine	routine
responsibility	responsabilité	royal	royal
rest (remainder)	reste	royalist	royaliste
restaurant	restaurant	ruin (n.)	ruine
restore	restaurer	ruin (v.)	ruiner
result (n.)	résultat	rum	rhum
result (v.)	résulter	rumor	rumeur
resume	résumé	rupture (n.)	rupture
retain	retenir	ruse	ruse
retard	retarder	rustic	rustique
retrace	retracer		
retreat (n.)	retraite	sabre	sabre
reunion	réunion	sack	sac
reunite	réunir	sacred	sacré

sacrifice	sacrifice	separate (*v.*)	séparer
sacrifice (*v.*)	sacrifier	separately	séparément
saint	saint	separation	séparation
salad	salade	serene	serein
salary	salaire	serenity	sérénité
salutary	salutaire	sergeant	sergent
sanction (*n.*)	sanction	series	série
sarcasm	sarcasme	serious	sérieux
satin	satin	seriously	sérieusement
satisfaction	satisfaction	sermon	sermon
satisfied	satisfait	serpent	serpent
sauce	sauce	servant	servante
savage	sauvage	serve	servir
scandal	scandale	service	service
scandalize	scandaliser	servile	servile
scandalous	scandaleux	servitude	servitude
scene	scène	session	session
sceptic	sceptique	severe	sévère
science	science	severely	sévèrement
scientific	scientifique	severity	sévérité
scruple	scrupule	sex	sexe
sculpture (*n.*)	sculpture	sign (*v.*)	signer
sculpture (*v.*)	sculpter	signal	signal
second (*adj.*)	second	signature	signature
second (*n.*)	seconde	signification	signification
secondary	secondaire	signify	signifier
secret (*adj.*)	secret	silence	silence
secret (*n.*)	secret	silhouette	silhouette
secretary	secrétaire	simple	simple
section	section	simplicity	simplicité
security	sécurité	simplify	simplifier
seduce	séduire	simply	simplement
seduction	séduction	simultaneous	simultané
senate	sénat	sincere	sincère
senator	sénateur	sincerely	sincèrement
sense (*n.*)	sens	sincerity	sincérité
sensibility	sensibilité	singular	singulier
sensual	sensuel	sinister	sinistre
sentiment	sentiment	sire (*n.*)	sire
sentimental	sentimental	siren	sirène

situate	situer	statue	statue
situation	situation	statuette	statuette
six	six	statute	statut
slave (n.)	esclave	sterile	stérile
sobriety	sobriété	stomach	estomac
social	social	strangle	étrangler
socialist	socialiste	strictly	strictement
society	société	structure	structure
solemnity	solennité	study (v.)	étudier
solicit	solliciter	stupefaction	stupéfaction
solicitude	sollicitude	stupefied	stupéfait
solid	solide	stupid	stupide
solidarity	solidarité	stupor	stupeur
solidity	solidité	style (n.)	style
solitary	solitaire	subject	sujet
solitude	solitude	sublime	sublime
solution	solution	submerge	submerger
sonorous	sonore	subordinate	subordonner
sophism	sophisme	subsist	subsister
soup	soupe	substitute (n.)	substitut
source	source	substitute (v.)	substituer
sovereign	souverain	substitution	substitution
space (n.)	espace	subterranean	souterrain
special	spécial	subtle	subtil
specially	spécialement	subvention	subvention
specialty	spécialité	success	succès
spectacle	spectacle	succession	succession
spectre	spectre	successive	successif
speculation	spéculation	successively	successivement
sphere	sphère	successor	successeur
spiral (n.)	spirale	succumb	succomber
spiritual	spirituel	suffice	suffire
splendid	splendide	sufficient	suffisant
splendor	splendeur	suffocate	suffoquer
sponge	éponge	suggest	suggérer
spontaneous	spontané	suggestion	suggestion
sport	sport	suicide	suicide
sportive	sportif	suite	suite
station	station	summit	sommet
statistic	statistique	sumptuous	somptueux

superb	superbe	tap (*v.*)	taper
superfluous	superflu	tapestry	tapisserie
superior	supérieur	tariff	tarif
superiority	supériorité	technique	technique
superstition	superstition	telegram (*n.*)	télégramme
supper (*n.*)	souper	telegraph (*n.*)	télégraphe
supple	souple	telegraph (*v.*)	télégraphier
supplementary	supplémentaire	telephone (*n.*)	téléphone
support (*v.*)	supporter	temperament	tempérament
suppose	supposer	temperature	température
supposition	supposition	tempest	tempête
suppression	suppression	temple	temple
supreme	suprême	tenacious	tenace
sure	sûr	tender (*adj.*)	tendre
surely	sûrement	tenebrous	ténébreux
surety	sûreté	tennis	tennis
surface (*n.*)	surface	tension	tension
surmount	surmonter	tent	tente
surpass	surpasser	terminate	terminer
surplus	surplus	terrace	terrasse
surprise (*n.*)	surprise	terrestrial	terrestre
surprised	surpris	terrible	terrible
surveillance	surveillance	terribly	terriblement
survive	survivre	terrify	terrifier
susceptible	susceptible	territory	territoire
suspend	suspendre	terror	terreur
suspension	suspension	testament	testament
syllable	syllable	text	texte
symbol	symbole	theatre	théâtre
symptom	symptôme	theme	thème
syndicate (*n.*)	syndicat	theology	théologie
syrup	sirop	theory	théorie
system	système	throne	trône
systematic	systématique	tiger	tigre
		timid	timide
table	table	timidity	timidité
tact	tact	tissue	tissu
tactics	tactique	tobacco	tabac
talent	talent	toilet	toilette
tambour	tambour	tolerate	tolérer

tomb	tombe	triumphant	triomphant
ton	tonne	trot	trotter
tone	ton	trouble (n.)	trouble
torment (n.)	tourment	trouble (v.)	troubler
torment (v.)	tourmenter	troupe	troupe
torrent	torrent	tube	tube
torture (n.)	torture	tumult	tumulte
torture (v.)	torturer	tunic	tunique
total	total	tunnel	tunnel
totally	totalement	turn (v.)	tourner
touching	touchant	type (n.)	type
tour (n.)	tour	tyranny	tyrannie
tourist	touriste	tyrant	tyran
trace (v.)	tracer		
tradition	tradition	unanimous	unanime
traditional	traditionnel	uncertain	incertain
tragedy	tragédie	uncle	oncle
tragic	tragique	uniform (adj.)	uniforme
train (n.)	train	union	union
trait	trait	unite	unir
tranquil	tranquille	united	uni
tranquility	tranquillité	unity	unité
transform	transformer	universal	universel
transformation	transformation	universe	univers
transition	transition	university (adj.)	universitaire
transmit	transmettre	university (n.)	université
transparent	transparent	unjust	injuste
transport (n.)	transport	unstable	instable
transport (v.)	transporter	urgent	urgent
traverse (v.)	traverser	usage	usage
treasure (n.)	trésor	use (v.)	user
tremble	trembler	usual	usuel
trembling (n.)	tremblement	usury	usure
tribe	tribu	utility	utilité
tribunal	tribunal	utilization	utilisation
tribune	tribune	utilize	utiliser
tricolored	tricolore		
triple (adj.)	triple	vacant	vacant
triumph (n.)	triomphe	vacation	vacances
triumph (v.)	triompher	vacillate	vaciller

vagabond	vagabond	vigilance	vigilance
vague	vague	vigor	vigeur
vainly	vainement	vigorous	vigoureux
valet	valet	villa	villa
valiant	vaillant	village	village
valise	valise	villain	vilain
valley	vallée	violation	violation
vanity	vanité	violence	violence
vapor	vapeur	violent	violent
variable	variable	violently	violemment
variation	variation	violet	violette
variety	variété	violin	violin
vary	varier	visible	visible
vase	vase	vision	vision
vassal	vassal	visit (n.)	visite
vast	vaste	visit (v.)	visiter
vegetable (adj.)	végétal	visitor	visiteur
vehemence	véhémence	vivacity	vivacité
vehicle	véhicule	vocation	vocation
vein	veine	volt	volt
vendor	vendeur	volume	volume
venerable	vénérable	voluntary	volontaire
venerate	vénérer	vote (n.)	vote
veneration	vénération	vote (v.)	voter
vengeance	vengeance	voyage (n.)	voyage
verdure	verdure	voyager	voyageur
verify	vérifier	vulgar	vulgaire
verse	vers	west	ouest
version	version		
vibrate	vibrer	zeal	zèle
vice	vice	zero	zéro
victim	victime	zinc	zinc
victory	victoire	zone	zone

A Glossary of Grammatical Terms

E. F. BLEILER

This section is intended to refresh your memory of grammatical terms or to clear up difficulties you may have had in understanding them. Before you work through the grammar, you should have a reasonably clear idea what the parts of speech and parts of a sentence are. This is not for reasons of pedantry, but simply because it is easier to talk about grammar if we agree upon terms. Grammatical terminology is as necessary to the study of grammar as the names of automobile parts are to garagemen.

This list is not exhaustive, and the definitions do not pretend to be complete, or to settle points of interpretation that grammarians have been disputing for the past several hundred years. It is a working analysis rather than a scholarly investigation. The definitions given, however, represent most typical American usage, and should serve for basic use.

The Parts of Speech

English words can be divided into eight important groups: nouns, adjectives, articles, verbs, adverbs, pronouns, prepositions, and conjunctions. The boundaries between one group of words and another are sometimes vague and ill-felt in English, but a good dictionary, like the Webster Collegiate, can help you make decisions in questionable cases. Always bear in mind, however, that the way a word is used in a sentence may be just as important as the nature of the word itself in deciding what part of speech the word is.

Nouns. *Nouns* are the *words* for *things* of all *sorts*, whether these *things* are real *objects* that you can see, or *ideas*, or *places*, or *qualities*, or *groups*, or more abstract *things*. *Examples* of *words* that are *nouns* are *cat, vase, door, shrub, wheat, university, mercy, intelligence, ocean, plumber, pleasure, society, army*.   If you are in *doubt* whether a given *word* is a *noun*, try putting the *word* "my," or "this," or "large" (or some other *adjective*) in *front* of it.   If it makes *sense* in the *sentence* the *chances* are that the *word* in *question* is a *noun*.   [All the *words* in *italics* in this *paragraph* are *nouns*.]

Adjectives.   Adjectives are the words which delimit or give you *specific* information about the *various* nouns in a sentence.   They tell you size, color, weight, pleasantness, and many *other* qualities.   *Such* words as *big, expensive, terrible, insipid, hot, delightful, ruddy, informative* are all *clear* adjectives.   If you are in *any* doubt whether a *certain* word is an adjective, add -er to it, or put the word "more" or "too" in front of it.   If it makes *good* sense in the sentence, and does not end in -ly, the chances are that it is an adjective.   (Pronoun-adjectives will be described under pronouns.)   [The adjectives in the *above* sentences are in italics.]

Articles.   There are only two kinds of articles in English, and they are easy to remember.   The definite article is "the" and the indefinite article is "a" or "an."

Verbs.   Verbs *are* the words that *tell* what action, or condition, or relationship *is going* on.   Such words as *was, is, jumps, achieved, keeps, buys, sells, has finished, run, will have, may, should pay, indicates are* all verb forms.   *Observe* that a verb *can be composed* of more than one word, as *will have* and *should pay*, above; these *are called* compound verbs.   As a rough guide for verbs, *try adding* -ed to the word you *are wondering* about, or *taking* off an -ed that *is* already there.   If it *makes* sense, the chances *are* that it *is* a verb.   (This *does* not always *work*, since the so-called strong or irregular verbs *make* forms by *changing* their middle vowels, like *spring, sprang, sprung*.)   [Verbs in this paragraph *are* in italics.]

Adverbs.   An adverb is a word that supplies additional information about a verb, an adjective, or another adverb.   It *usually* indicates time, or manner, or place, or degree.   It tells you *how*, or *when*, or *where*, or to what degree things are happening.

Such words as *now, then, there, not, anywhere, never, somehow, always, very,* and most words ending in -ly are *ordinarily* adverbs. [Italicized words are adverbs.]

Pronouns.   Pronouns are related to nouns, and take their place. (Some grammars and dictionaries group pronouns and nouns together as substantives.) *They* mention persons, or objects of any sort without actually giving their names.

There are several different kinds of pronouns. (1) Personal pronouns: by a grammatical convention *I, we, me, mine, us, ours* are called first person pronouns, since *they* refer to the speaker; *you* and *yours* are called second person pronouns, since *they* refer to the person addressed; and *he, him, his, she, her, hers, they, them, theirs* are called third person pronouns since *they* refer to the things or persons discussed. (2) Demonstrative pronouns: *this, that, these, those.* (3) Interrogative, or question, pronouns: *who, whom, what, whose, which.* (4) Relative pronouns, or pronouns *which* refer back to something already mentioned: *who, whom, that, which.* (5) Others: *some, any, anyone, no one, other, whichever, none,* etc.

Pronouns are difficult for *us,* since our categories are not as clear as in some other languages, and *we* use the same words for *what* foreign-language speakers see as different situations. First, our interrogative and relative pronouns overlap, and must be separated in translation. The easiest way is to observe whether a question is involved in the sentence. Examples: "*Which* [int.] do *you* like?" "The inn, *which* [rel.] was not far from Cadiz, had a restaurant." "*Who* [int.] is there?" "*I* don't know *who* [int.] was there." "The porter *who* [rel.] took our bags was Number 2132." *This* may seem to be a trivial difference to an English speaker, but in some languages *it* is very important.

Secondly, there is an overlap between pronouns and adjectives. In some cases the word "this," for example, is a pronoun; in other cases *it* is an adjective. *This* also holds true for *his, its, her, any, none, other, some, that, these, those,* and many other words. Note whether the word in question stands alone or is associated with another word. Examples: "*This* [pronoun] is mine." "This [adj.] taxi has no springs." Watch out for the word "that," which can be a pronoun or an adjective or a conjunction. And remember that "my," "your," "our," and "their" are always adjectives. [All pronouns in this section are in italics.]

Prepositions. Prepositions are the little words that introduce phrases that tell *about* condition, time, place, manner, association, degree, and similar topics. Such words as *with, in, beside, under, of, to, about, for,* and *upon* are prepositions. In English prepositions and adverbs overlap, but, as you will see *by* checking *in* your dictionary, there are usually differences *of* meaning *between* the two uses. [Prepositions *in* this paragraph are designated *by* italics.]

Conjunctions. Conjunctions are joining-words. They enable you to link words *or* groups of words into larger units, *and* to build compound *or* complex sentences out of simple sentence units. Such words as *and, but, although, or, unless,* are typical conjunctions. *Although* most conjunctions are easy enough to identify, the word "that" should be watched closely to see *that* it is not a pronoun *or* an adjective. [Conjunctions italicized.]

Words about Verbs

Verbs are responsible for most of the terminology in this short grammar. The basic terms are:

Conjugation. In many languages verbs fall into natural groups, according to the way they make their forms. These groupings are called conjugations, and are an aid to learning grammatical structure. Though it may seem difficult at first to speak of First and Second Conjugations, these are simply short ways of saying that verbs belonging to these classes make their forms according to certain consistent rules, which you can memorize.

Infinitive. This is the basic form which most dictionaries give for verbs in most languages, and in most languages it serves as the basis for classifying verbs. In English (with a very few exceptions) it has no special form. To find the infinitive for any English verb, just fill in this sentence: "I like to......... (walk, run, jump, swim, carry, disappear, etc.)." The infinitive in English is usually preceded by the word "to."

Tense. This is simply a formal way of saying "time." In English we think of time as being broken into three great segments: past, present, and future. Our verbs are assigned forms to indicate this division, and are further subdivided for shades of meaning. We subdivide the present time into the present (I walk) and present progressive (I am walking); the past into the simple past (I walked), progressive past (I was walking), perfect or present perfect (I have walked), past perfect or pluperfect (I had walked); and future into simple future (I shall walk) and future progressive (I shall be walking). These are the most common English tenses.

Present Participles, Progressive Tenses. In English the present participle always ends in -*ing*. It can be used as a noun or an adjective in some situations, but its chief use is in *forming* the so-called progressive tenses. These are made by *putting* appropriate forms of the verb "to be" before a present participle: In "to walk" [an infinitive], for example, the present progressive would be: I am *walking*, you are *walking*, he is *walking*, etc.; past progressive, I was *walking*, you were *walking*, and so on. [Present participles are in italics.]

Past Participles, Perfect Tenses. The past participle in English is not *formed* as regularly as is the present participle. Sometimes it is *constructed* by adding -ed or -d to the present tense, as *walked, jumped, looked, received*; but there are many verbs where it is *formed* less regularly: *seen, been, swum, chosen, brought*. To find it, simply fill out the sentence "I have ...." putting in the verb form that your ear tells you is right for the particular verb. If you speak grammatically, you will have the past participle.

Past participles are sometimes used as adjectives: "Don't cry over *spilt* milk." Their most important use, however, is to form the system of verb tenses that are *called* the perfect tenses: present perfect (or perfect), past perfect (or pluperfect), etc. In English the present perfect tense is *formed* with the present tense of "to have" and the past participle of a verb: I have *walked*, you have *run*, he has *begun*, etc. The past perfect is *formed*, similarly, with the past tense of "to have" and the past participle: I had *walked*, you had *run*, he had *begun*. Most of the languages you are likely to study have similar systems of perfect tenses, though they may not be *formed* in exactly the same way as in English. [Past participles in italics.]

Preterit, Imperfect. Many languages have more than one verb tense for expressing an action that took place in the past. They may use a perfect tense (which we have just covered), or a preterit, or an imperfect. English, although you may never have thought about it, is one of these languages, for we can say "I have spoken to him" [present perfect], or "I spoke to him" [simple past], or "I was speaking to him" [past progressive]. These sentences do not mean exactly the same thing, although the differences are subtle, and are difficult to put into other words.

While usage differs a little from language to language, if a language has both a preterit and an imperfect, in general the preterit corresponds to the English simple past (I ran, I swam, I spoke), and the imperfect corresponds to the English past progressive (I was running, I was swimming, I was speaking). If you are curious to discover the mode of thought behind these different tenses, try looking at the situation in terms of background-action and point-action. One of the most important uses of the imperfect is to provide a background against which a single point-action can take place. For example, "When I was walking down the street [background, continued over a period of time, hence past progressive or imperfect], I stubbed my toe [an instant or point of time, hence a simple past or preterit]."

Auxiliary Verbs. Auxiliary verbs are special words that are used to help other verbs make their forms. In English, for example, we use forms of the verb to have to make our perfect tenses: I have seen, you had come, he has been, etc. We also use shall or will to make our future tenses: I shall pay, you will see, etc. French, German, Spanish, and Italian also make use of auxiliary verbs, but although the general concept is present, the use of auxiliaries differs very much from one language to another, and you must learn the practice for each language.

Reflexive. This term, which sounds more difficult than it really is, simply means that the verb flexes back upon the noun or pronoun that is its subject. In modern English the reflexive pronoun always has -*self* on its end, and we do not use the construction very frequently. In other languages, however, reflexive forms may be used more frequently, and in ways that do not seem very logical to an English speaker. Examples of English reflexive sentences: "He washes himself." "He seated himself at the table."

Passive. In some languages, like Latin, there is a strong feeling that an action or thing that is taking place can be expressed in two different ways. One can say, A does-something-to B, which is "active;" or B is-having-something-done-to-him by A, which is "passive." We do not have a strong feeling for this classification of experience in English, but the following examples should indicate the difference between an active and a passive verb: Active: "John is building a house." Passive: "A house is being built by John." Active: "The steamer carried the cotton to England." Passive: "The cotton was carried by the steamer to England." Bear in mind that the formation of passive verbs and the situations where they can be used vary enormously from language to language. This is one situation where you usually cannot translate English word for word into another language and make sense.

Impersonal Verbs. In English there are some verbs which do not have an ordinary subject, and do not refer to persons. They are always used with the pronoun *it*, which does not refer to anything specifically, but simply serves to fill out the verb forms. Examples: It is snowing. It hailed last night. It seems to me that you are wrong. It has been raining. It won't do.

Other languages, like German, have this same general concept, but impersonal verbs may differ quite a bit in form and frequency from one language to another.

Words about Nouns

Agreement.   In some languages, where nouns or adjectives or articles are declined, or have gender endings, it is necessary that the adjective or article be in the same case or gender or number as the noun it goes with (modifies). This is called agreement.

This may be illustrated from Spanish, where articles and adjectives have to agree with nouns in gender and number.

| una casa blanca | one white house | dos casas blancas | two white houses |
| un libro blanco | one white book | dos libros blancos | two white books |

Here *una* is feminine singular and has the ending -*a* because it agrees with the feminine singular noun *casa*; *blanca* has the ending -*a* because it agrees with the feminine singular noun *casa*. *blanco*, on the other hand, and *un*, are masculine singular because *libro* is masculine singular.

Gender.   Gender should not be confused with actual sex. In many languages nouns are arbitrarily assigned a gender (masculine or feminine, or masculine or feminine or neuter), and this need not correspond to sex. You simply have to learn the pattern of the language you are studying in order to become familiar with its use of gender.

Miscellaneous Terms

Comparative, Superlative.   These two terms are used with adjectives and adverbs. They indicate the degree of strength within the meaning of the word. Faster, better, earlier, newer, more rapid, more detailed, more suitable are examples of the comparative in adjectives, while more rapidly, more recently, more suitably are comparatives for adverbs. In most cases, as you have seen, the comparative uses -er or "more" for an adjective, and "more" for an adverb. Superlatives are those forms which end in -est or have "most" prefixed before them for adjectives, and "most" prefixed for adverbs: most intelligent, earliest, most rapidly, most suitably.

Idiom. An idiom is an expression that is peculiar to a language, the meaning of which is not the same as the literal meaning of the individual words composing it. Idioms, as a rule, cannot be translated word by word into another language. Examples of English idioms: "*Take it easy.*" Don't *beat around the bush.*" "It *turned out* to be *a Dutch treat.*" "Can you *tell time* in Spanish?"

The Parts of the Sentence

Subject, Predicate. In grammar *every complete sentence* contains two basic parts, the subject and the predicate. *The subject,* if *we* state the terms most simply, is the thing, person, or activity talked about. *It* can be a noun, a pronoun, or something *that* serves as a noun. *A subject* would include, in a typical case, a noun, the articles or adjectives *which* are associated with it, and perhaps phrases. Note that in complex sentences, *each part* may have its own subject. [*The subjects of the sentences above* have been italicized.]

The predicate *talks about the subject.* In a formal sentence the predicate *includes a verb, its adverbs, predicate adjectives, phrases, and objects*—whatever *happens to be present.* A predicate adjective *is an adjective* which *happens to be in the predicate after a form of the verb to be.* Example: "Apples *are red.*" [Predicates *are in italics.*]

In the following simple sentences subjects are in italics, predicates in italics and underlined. *"Green apples are bad for your digestion."* "When *I go to Spain, I always stop in Cadiz."* "*The man with the handbag is travelling to Madrid.*"

Direct and Indirect Objects. Some verbs (called transitive verbs) take direct and/or indirect objects in their predicates; other verbs (called intransitive verbs) do not take objects of any sort. In English, except for pronouns, objects do not have any special forms, but in languages which have case forms or more pronoun forms than English, objects can be troublesome.

The direct object is the person, thing, quality, or matter that the verb directs *its action* upon. It can be a pronoun, or a noun, perhaps accompanied by an article and/or adjectives. The direct object always directly follows *its verb*, except when there is also an indirect object pronoun present, which comes between the verb and the object. Prepositions do not go before direct objects. Examples: "The cook threw *green onions* into the stew." "The border guards will want to see *your passport* tomorrow." "Give *it* to me." "Please give me *a glass of red wine.*" [We have placed *direct objects* in this paragraph in italics.]

The indirect object, as grammars will tell *you*, is the person or thing for or to whom the action is taking place. It can be a pronoun or a noun with or without article and adjectives. In most cases the words "to" or "for" can be inserted before it, if not already there. Examples: "Please tell *me* the time." "I wrote *her* a letter from Barcelona." "We sent *Mr. Gonzalez* ten pesos." "We gave *the most energetic guide* a large tip." [Indirect objects are in italics.]

INDEX

The following abbreviations have been used in this index: *conj.* for conjugation and *def.* for definition. French words appear in *italics* and their English translations in parentheses.

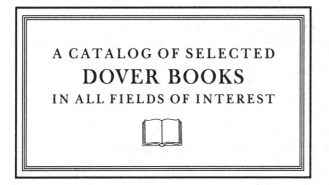

A CATALOG OF SELECTED

DOVER BOOKS

IN ALL FIELDS OF INTEREST

A CATALOG OF SELECTED DOVER
BOOKS IN ALL FIELDS OF INTEREST

CONCERNING THE SPIRITUAL IN ART, Wassily Kandinsky. Pioneering work by father of abstract art. Thoughts on color theory, nature of art. Analysis of earlier masters. 12 illustrations. 80pp. of text. 5⅜ x 8½.   0-486-23411-8

CELTIC ART: The Methods of Construction, George Bain. Simple geometric techniques for making Celtic interlacements, spirals, Kells-type initials, animals, humans, etc. Over 500 illustrations. 160pp. 9 x 12. (Available in U.S. only.)   0-486-22923-8

AN ATLAS OF ANATOMY FOR ARTISTS, Fritz Schider. Most thorough reference work on art anatomy in the world. Hundreds of illustrations, including selections from works by Vesalius, Leonardo, Goya, Ingres, Michelangelo, others. 593 illustrations. 192pp. 7⅛ x 10¼.   0-486-20241-0

CELTIC HAND STROKE-BY-STROKE (Irish Half-Uncial from "The Book of Kells"): An Arthur Baker Calligraphy Manual, Arthur Baker. Complete guide to creating each letter of the alphabet in distinctive Celtic manner. Covers hand position, strokes, pens, inks, paper, more. Illustrated. 48pp. 8¼ x 11.   0-486-24336-2

EASY ORIGAMI, John Montroll. Charming collection of 32 projects (hat, cup, pelican, piano, swan, many more) specially designed for the novice origami hobbyist. Clearly illustrated easy-to-follow instructions insure that even beginning papercrafters will achieve successful results. 48pp. 8¼ x 11.   0-486-27298-2

BLOOMINGDALE'S ILLUSTRATED 1886 CATALOG: Fashions, Dry Goods and Housewares, Bloomingdale Brothers. Famed merchants' extremely rare catalog depicting about 1,700 products: clothing, housewares, firearms, dry goods, jewelry, more. Invaluable for dating, identifying vintage items. Also, copyright-free graphics for artists, designers. Co-published with Henry Ford Museum & Greenfield Village. 160pp. 8¼ x 11.   0-486-25780-0

THE ART OF WORLDLY WISDOM, Baltasar Gracian. "Think with the few and speak with the many," "Friends are a second existence," and "Be able to forget" are among this 1637 volume's 300 pithy maxims. A perfect source of mental and spiritual refreshment, it can be opened at random and appreciated either in brief or at length. 128pp. 5⅜ x 8½.   0-486-44034-6

JOHNSON'S DICTIONARY: A Modern Selection, Samuel Johnson (E. L. McAdam and George Milne, eds.). This modern version reduces the original 1755 edition's 2,300 pages of definitions and literary examples to a more manageable length, retaining the verbal pleasure and historical curiosity of the original. 480pp. 5³⁄₁₆ x 8¼.   0-486-44089-3

ADVENTURES OF HUCKLEBERRY FINN, Mark Twain, Illustrated by E. W. Kemble. A work of eternal richness and complexity, a source of ongoing critical debate, and a literary landmark, Twain's 1885 masterpiece about a barefoot boy's journey of self-discovery has enthralled readers around the world. This handsome clothbound reproduction of the first edition features all 174 of the original black-and-white illustrations. 368pp. 5⅜ x 8½.   0-486-44322-1

THE CLARINET AND CLARINET PLAYING, David Pino. Lively, comprehensive work features suggestions about technique, musicianship, and musical interpretation, as well as guidelines for teaching, making your own reeds, and preparing for public performance. Includes an intriguing look at clarinet history. "A godsend," *The Clarinet,* Journal of the International Clarinet Society. Appendixes. 7 illus. 320pp. 5⅜ x 8½. 0-486-40270-3

HOLLYWOOD GLAMOR PORTRAITS, John Kobal (ed.). 145 photos from 1926-49. Harlow, Gable, Bogart, Bacall; 94 stars in all. Full background on photographers, technical aspects. 160pp. 8⅜ x 11¼. 0-486-23352-9

THE RAVEN AND OTHER FAVORITE POEMS, Edgar Allan Poe. Over 40 of the author's most memorable poems: "The Bells," "Ulalume," "Israfel," "To Helen," "The Conqueror Worm," "Eldorado," "Annabel Lee," many more. Alphabetic lists of titles and first lines. 64pp. 5 3/16 x 8¼. 0-486-26685-0

PERSONAL MEMOIRS OF U. S. GRANT, Ulysses Simpson Grant. Intelligent, deeply moving firsthand account of Civil War campaigns, considered by many the finest military memoirs ever written. Includes letters, historic photographs, maps and more. 528pp. 6⅛ x 9¼. 0-486-28587-1

POE ILLUSTRATED: Art by Doré, Dulac, Rackham and Others, selected and edited by Jeff A. Menges. More than 100 compelling illustrations, in brilliant color and crisp black-and-white, include scenes from "The Raven," "The Pit and the Pendulum," "The Gold-Bug," and other stories and poems. 96pp. 8⅜ x 11. 0-486-45746-X

RUSSIAN STORIES/RUSSKIE RASSKAZY: A Dual-Language Book, edited by Gleb Struve. Twelve tales by such masters as Chekhov, Tolstoy, Dostoevsky, Pushkin, others. Excellent word-for-word English translations on facing pages, plus teaching and study aids, Russian/English vocabulary, biographical/critical introductions, more. 416pp. 5⅜ x 8½. 0-486-26244-8

PHILADELPHIA THEN AND NOW: 60 Sites Photographed in the Past and Present, Kenneth Finkel and Susan Oyama. Rare photographs of City Hall, Logan Square, Independence Hall, Betsy Ross House, other landmarks juxtaposed with contemporary views. Captures changing face of historic city. Introduction. Captions. 128pp. 8¼ x 11. 0-486-25790-8

NORTH AMERICAN INDIAN LIFE: Customs and Traditions of 23 Tribes, Elsie Clews Parsons (ed.). 27 fictionalized essays by noted anthropologists examine religion, customs, government, additional facets of life among the Winnebago, Crow, Zuni, Eskimo, other tribes. 480pp. 6⅛ x 9¼. 0-486-27377-6

TECHNICAL MANUAL AND DICTIONARY OF CLASSICAL BALLET, Gail Grant. Defines, explains, comments on steps, movements, poses and concepts. 15-page pictorial section. Basic book for student, viewer. 127pp. 5⅜ x 8½. 0-486-21843-0

THE MALE AND FEMALE FIGURE IN MOTION: 60 Classic Photographic Sequences, Eadweard Muybridge. 60 true-action photographs of men and women walking, running, climbing, bending, turning, etc., reproduced from a rare 19th-century masterpiece. vi + 121pp. 9 x 12. 0-486-24745-7

ANIMALS: 1,419 Copyright-Free Illustrations of Mammals, Birds, Fish, Insects, etc., Jim Harter (ed.). Clear wood engravings present, in extremely lifelike poses, over 1,000 species of animals. One of the most extensive pictorial sourcebooks of its kind. Captions. Index. 284pp. 9 x 12. 0-486-23766-4

1001 QUESTIONS ANSWERED ABOUT THE SEASHORE, N. J. Berrill and Jacquelyn Berrill. Queries answered about dolphins, sea snails, sponges, starfish, fishes, shore birds, many others. Covers appearance, breeding, growth, feeding, much more. 305pp. 5¼ x 8¼. 0-486-23366-9

ATTRACTING BIRDS TO YOUR YARD, William J. Weber. Easy-to-follow guide offers advice on how to attract the greatest diversity of birds: birdhouses, feeders, water and waterers, much more. 96pp. 5³⁄₁₆ x 8¼. 0-486-28927-3

MEDICINAL AND OTHER USES OF NORTH AMERICAN PLANTS: A Historical Survey with Special Reference to the Eastern Indian Tribes, Charlotte Erichsen-Brown. Chronological historical citations document 500 years of usage of plants, trees, shrubs native to eastern Canada, northeastern U.S. Also complete identifying information. 343 illustrations. 544pp. 6½ x 9¼. 0-486-25951-X

STORYBOOK MAZES, Dave Phillips. 23 stories and mazes on two-page spreads: Wizard of Oz, Treasure Island, Robin Hood, etc. Solutions. 64pp. 8¼ x 11.
0-486-23628-5

AMERICAN NEGRO SONGS: 230 Folk Songs and Spirituals, Religious and Secular, John W. Work. This authoritative study traces the African influences of songs sung and played by black Americans at work, in church, and as entertainment. The author discusses the lyric significance of such songs as "Swing Low, Sweet Chariot," "John Henry," and others and offers the words and music for 230 songs. Bibliography. Index of Song Titles. 272pp. 6½ x 9¼. 0-486-40271-1

MOVIE-STAR PORTRAITS OF THE FORTIES, John Kobal (ed.). 163 glamor, studio photos of 106 stars of the 1940s: Rita Hayworth, Ava Gardner, Marlon Brando, Clark Gable, many more. 176pp. 8⅜ x 11¼. 0-486-23546-7

YEKL and THE IMPORTED BRIDEGROOM AND OTHER STORIES OF YIDDISH NEW YORK, Abraham Cahan. Film Hester Street based on *Yekl* (1896). Novel, other stories among first about Jewish immigrants on N.Y.'s East Side. 240pp. 5⅜ x 8½. 0-486-22427-9

SELECTED POEMS, Walt Whitman. Generous sampling from *Leaves of Grass*. Twenty-four poems include "I Hear America Singing," "Song of the Open Road," "I Sing the Body Electric," "When Lilacs Last in the Dooryard Bloom'd," "O Captain! My Captain!"–all reprinted from an authoritative edition. Lists of titles and first lines. 128pp. 5³⁄₁₆ x 8¼. 0-486-26878-0

SONGS OF EXPERIENCE: Facsimile Reproduction with 26 Plates in Full Color, William Blake. 26 full-color plates from a rare 1826 edition. Includes "The Tyger," "London," "Holy Thursday," and other poems. Printed text of poems. 48pp. 5¼ x 7.
0-486-24636-1

THE BEST TALES OF HOFFMANN, E. T. A. Hoffmann. 10 of Hoffmann's most important stories: "Nutcracker and the King of Mice," "The Golden Flowerpot," etc. 458pp. 5⅜ x 8½. 0-486-21793-0

THE BOOK OF TEA, Kakuzo Okakura. Minor classic of the Orient: entertaining, charming explanation, interpretation of traditional Japanese culture in terms of tea ceremony. 94pp. 5⅜ x 8½. 0-486-20070-1

FRENCH STORIES/CONTES FRANÇAIS: A Dual-Language Book, Wallace Fowlie. Ten stories by French masters, Voltaire to Camus: "Micromegas" by Voltaire; "The Atheist's Mass" by Balzac; "Minuet" by de Maupassant; "The Guest" by Camus, six more. Excellent English translations on facing pages. Also French-English vocabulary list, exercises, more. 352pp. 5⅜ x 8½.   0-486-26443-2

CHICAGO AT THE TURN OF THE CENTURY IN PHOTOGRAPHS: 122 Historic Views from the Collections of the Chicago Historical Society, Larry A. Viskochil. Rare large-format prints offer detailed views of City Hall, State Street, the Loop, Hull House, Union Station, many other landmarks, circa 1904-1913. Introduction. Captions. Maps. 144pp. 9⅜ x 12¼.   0-486-24656-6

OLD BROOKLYN IN EARLY PHOTOGRAPHS, 1865–1929, William Lee Younger. Luna Park, Gravesend race track, construction of Grand Army Plaza, moving of Hotel Brighton, etc. 157 previously unpublished photographs. 165pp. 8⅞ x 11¾.   0-486-23587-4

THE MYTHS OF THE NORTH AMERICAN INDIANS, Lewis Spence. Rich anthology of the myths and legends of the Algonquins, Iroquois, Pawnees and Sioux, prefaced by an extensive historical and ethnological commentary. 36 illustrations. 480pp. 5⅜ x 8½.   0-486-25967-6

AN ENCYCLOPEDIA OF BATTLES: Accounts of Over 1,560 Battles from 1479 B.C. to the Present, David Eggenberger. Essential details of every major battle in recorded history from the first battle of Megiddo in 1479 B.C. to Grenada in 1984. List of Battle Maps. New Appendix covering the years 1967–1984. Index. 99 illustrations. 544pp. 6½ x 9¼.   0-486-24913-1

SAILING ALONE AROUND THE WORLD, Captain Joshua Slocum. First man to sail around the world, alone, in small boat. One of the great feats of seamanship told in delightful manner. 67 illustrations. 294pp. 5⅜ x 8½.   0-486-20326-3

ANARCHISM AND OTHER ESSAYS, Emma Goldman. Powerful, penetrating, prophetic essays on direct action, role of minorities, prison reform, puritan hypocrisy, violence, etc. 271pp. 5⅜ x 8½.   0-486-22484-8

MYTHS OF THE HINDUS AND BUDDHISTS, Ananda K. Coomaraswamy and Sister Nivedita. Great stories of the epics; deeds of Krishna, Shiva, taken from puranas, Vedas, folk tales; etc. 32 illustrations. 400pp. 5⅜ x 8½.   0-486-21759-0

MY BONDAGE AND MY FREEDOM, Frederick Douglass. Born a slave, Douglass became outspoken force in antislavery movement. The best of Douglass' autobiographies. Graphic description of slave life. 464pp. 5⅜ x 8½.   0-486-22457-0

FOLLOWING THE EQUATOR: A Journey Around the World, Mark Twain. Fascinating humorous account of 1897 voyage to Hawaii, Australia, India, New Zealand, etc. Ironic, bemused reports on peoples, customs, climate, flora and fauna, politics, much more. 197 illustrations. 720pp. 5⅜ x 8½.   0-486-26113-1

GREAT SPEECHES BY AMERICAN WOMEN, edited by James Daley. Here are 21 legendary speeches from the country's most inspirational female voices, including Sojourner Truth, Susan B. Anthony, Eleanor Roosevelt, Hillary Rodham Clinton, Nancy Pelosi, and many others. 192pp. 5³⁄₁₆ x 8¼.   0-486-46141-6

THE MYTHS OF GREECE AND ROME, H. A. Guerber. A classic of mythology, generously illustrated, long prized for its simple, graphic, accurate retelling of the principal myths of Greece and Rome, and for its commentary on their origins and significance. With 64 illustrations by Michelangelo, Raphael, Titian, Rubens, Canova, Bernini and others. 480pp. 5⅜ x 8½.   0-486-27584-1

HOW TO DO BEADWORK, Mary White. Fundamental book on craft from simple projects to five-bead chains and woven works. 106 illustrations. 142pp. 5⅜ x 8.
0-486-20697-1

THE 1912 AND 1915 GUSTAV STICKLEY FURNITURE CATALOGS, Gustav Stickley. With over 200 detailed illustrations and descriptions, these two catalogs are essential reading and reference materials and identification guides for Stickley furniture. Captions cite materials, dimensions and prices. 112pp. 6½ x 9¼. 0-486-26676-1

SIX GREAT DIALOGUES: Apology, Crito, Phaedo, Phaedrus, Symposium, The Republic, Plato, translated by Benjamin Jowett. Plato's Dialogues rank among Western civilization's most important and influential philosophical works. These 6 selections of his major works explore a broad range of enduringly relevant issues. Authoritative Jowett translations. 480pp. 5³⁄₁₆ x 8¼. 0-486-45465-7

DEMONOLATRY: An Account of the Historical Practice of Witchcraft, Nicolas Remy, edited with an Introduction and Notes by Montague Summers, translated by E. A. Ashwin. This extremely influential 1595 study was frequently cited at witchcraft trials. In addition to lurid details of satanic pacts and sexual perversity, it presents the particulars of numerous court cases. 240pp. 6½ x 9¼. 0-486-46137-8

VICTORIAN FASHIONS AND COSTUMES FROM HARPER'S BAZAAR, 1867–1898, Stella Blum (ed.). Day costumes, evening wear, sports clothes, shoes, hats, other accessories in over 1,000 detailed engravings. 320pp. 9⅜ x 12¼.
0-486-22990-4

THE LONG ISLAND RAIL ROAD IN EARLY PHOTOGRAPHS, Ron Ziel. Over 220 rare photos, informative text document origin (1844) and development of rail service on Long Island. Vintage views of early trains, locomotives, stations, passengers, crews, much more. Captions. 8⅞ x 11¾. 0-486-26301-0

VOYAGE OF THE LIBERDADE, Joshua Slocum. Great 19th-century mariner's thrilling, first-hand account of the wreck of his ship off South America, the 35-foot boat he built from the wreckage, and its remarkable voyage home. 128pp. 5⅜ x 8½.
0-486-40022-0

TEN BOOKS ON ARCHITECTURE, Vitruvius. The most important book ever written on architecture. Early Roman aesthetics, technology, classical orders, site selection, all other aspects. Morgan translation. 331pp. 5⅜ x 8½. 0-486-20645-9

THE HUMAN FIGURE IN MOTION, Eadweard Muybridge. More than 4,500 stopped-action photos, in action series, showing undraped men, women, children jumping, lying down, throwing, sitting, wrestling, carrying, etc. 390pp. 7⅞ x 10⅝.
0-486-20204-6 Clothbd.

TREES OF THE EASTERN AND CENTRAL UNITED STATES AND CANADA, William M. Harlow. Best one-volume guide to 140 trees. Full descriptions, woodlore, range, etc. Over 600 illustrations. Handy size. 288pp. 4½ x 6⅜. 0-486-20395-6

MY FIRST BOOK OF TCHAIKOVSKY: Favorite Pieces in Easy Piano Arrangements, edited by David Dutkanicz. These special arrangements of favorite Tchaikovsky themes are ideal for beginner pianists, child or adult. Contents include themes from "The Nutcracker," "March Slav," Symphonies Nos. 5 and 6, "Swan Lake," "Sleeping Beauty," and more. 48pp. 8¼ x 11. 0-486-46416-4

BIG BOOK OF MAZES AND LABYRINTHS, Walter Shepherd. 50 mazes and labyrinths in all—classical, solid, ripple, and more—in one great volume. Perfect inexpensive puzzler for clever youngsters. Full solutions. 112pp. 8⅛ x 11. 0-486-22951-3

PIANO TUNING, J. Cree Fischer. Clearest, best book for beginner, amateur. Simple repairs, raising dropped notes, tuning by easy method of flattened fifths. No previous skills needed. 4 illustrations. 201pp. 5⅜ x 8½. 0-486-23267-0

HINTS TO SINGERS, Lillian Nordica. Selecting the right teacher, developing confidence, overcoming stage fright, and many other important skills receive thoughtful discussion in this indispensible guide, written by a world-famous diva of four decades' experience. 96pp. $5^3/_8$ x $8^1/_2$. 0-486-40094-8

THE COMPLETE NONSENSE OF EDWARD LEAR, Edward Lear. All nonsense limericks, zany alphabets, Owl and Pussycat, songs, nonsense botany, etc., illustrated by Lear. Total of 320pp. $5^3/_8$ x $8^1/_2$. (Available in U.S. only.) 0-486-20167-8

VICTORIAN PARLOUR POETRY: An Annotated Anthology, Michael R. Turner. 117 gems by Longfellow, Tennyson, Browning, many lesser-known poets. "The Village Blacksmith," "Curfew Must Not Ring Tonight," "Only a Baby Small," dozens more, often difficult to find elsewhere. Index of poets, titles, first lines. xxiii + 325pp. $5^5/_8$ x $8^1/_4$. 0-486-27044-0

DUBLINERS, James Joyce. Fifteen stories offer vivid, tightly focused observations of the lives of Dublin's poorer classes. At least one, "The Dead," is considered a masterpiece. Reprinted complete and unabridged from standard edition. 160pp. $5^3/_{16}$ x $8^1/_4$. 0-486-26870-5

THE LITTLE RED SCHOOLHOUSE, Eric Sloane. Harkening back to a time when the three Rs stood for reading, 'riting, and religion, Sloane's sketchbook explores the history of early American schools. Includes marvelous illustrations of one-room New England schoolhouses, desks, and benches. 48pp. $8^1/_4$ x 11. 0-486-45604-8

THE BOOK OF THE SACRED MAGIC OF ABRAMELIN THE MAGE, translated by S. MacGregor Mathers. Medieval manuscript of ceremonial magic. Basic document in Aleister Crowley, Golden Dawn groups. 268pp. $5^3/_8$ x $8^1/_2$. 0-486-23211-5

THE BATTLES THAT CHANGED HISTORY, Fletcher Pratt. Eminent historian profiles 16 crucial conflicts, ancient to modern, that changed the course of civilization. 352pp. $5^3/_8$ x $8^1/_2$. 0-486-41129-X

NEW RUSSIAN-ENGLISH AND ENGLISH-RUSSIAN DICTIONARY, M. A. O'Brien. This is a remarkably handy Russian dictionary, containing a surprising amount of information, including over 70,000 entries. 366pp. $4^1/_2$ x $6^1/_8$. 0-486-20208-9

NEW YORK IN THE FORTIES, Andreas Feininger. 162 brilliant photographs by the well-known photographer, formerly with *Life* magazine. Commuters, shoppers, Times Square at night, much else from city at its peak. Captions by John von Hartz. 181pp. $9^1/_4$ x $10^3/_4$. 0-486-23585-8

INDIAN SIGN LANGUAGE, William Tomkins. Over 525 signs developed by Sioux and other tribes. Written instructions and diagrams. Also 290 pictographs. 111pp. $6^1/_8$ x $9^1/_4$. 0-486-22029-X

ANATOMY: A Complete Guide for Artists, Joseph Sheppard. A master of figure drawing shows artists how to render human anatomy convincingly. Over 460 illustrations. 224pp. $8^3/_8$ x $11^1/_4$. 0-486-27279-6

MEDIEVAL CALLIGRAPHY: Its History and Technique, Marc Drogin. Spirited history, comprehensive instruction manual covers 13 styles (ca. 4th century through 15th). Excellent photographs; directions for duplicating medieval techniques with modern tools. 224pp. $8^3/_8$ x $11^1/_4$. 0-486-26142-5

DRIED FLOWERS: How to Prepare Them, Sarah Whitlock and Martha Rankin. Complete instructions on how to use silica gel, meal and borax, perlite aggregate, sand and borax, glycerine and water to create attractive permanent flower arrangements. 12 illustrations. 32pp. $5\frac{3}{8}$ x $8\frac{1}{2}$. 0-486-21802-3

EASY-TO-MAKE BIRD FEEDERS FOR WOODWORKERS, Scott D. Campbell. Detailed, simple-to-use guide for designing, constructing, caring for and using feeders. Text, illustrations for 12 classic and contemporary designs. 96pp. $5\frac{3}{8}$ x $8\frac{1}{2}$. 0-486-25847-5

THE COMPLETE BOOK OF BIRDHOUSE CONSTRUCTION FOR WOODWORKERS, Scott D. Campbell. Detailed instructions, illustrations, tables. Also data on bird habitat and instinct patterns. Bibliography. 3 tables. 63 illustrations in 15 figures. 48pp. $5\frac{1}{4}$ x $8\frac{1}{2}$. 0-486-24407-5

SCOTTISH WONDER TALES FROM MYTH AND LEGEND, Donald A. Mackenzie. 16 lively tales tell of giants rumbling down mountainsides, of a magic wand that turns stone pillars into warriors, of gods and goddesses, evil hags, powerful forces and more. 240pp. $5\frac{3}{8}$ x $8\frac{1}{2}$. 0-486-29677-6

THE HISTORY OF UNDERCLOTHES, C. Willett Cunnington and Phyllis Cunnington. Fascinating, well-documented survey covering six centuries of English undergarments, enhanced with over 100 illustrations: 12th-century laced-up bodice, footed long drawers (1795), 19th-century bustles, 19th-century corsets for men, Victorian "bust improvers," much more. 272pp. $5\frac{5}{8}$ x $8\frac{1}{4}$. 0-486-27124-2

FIRST FRENCH READER: A Beginner's Dual-Language Book, edited and translated by Stanley Appelbaum. This anthology introduces fifty legendary writers–Voltaire, Balzac, Baudelaire, Proust, more–through passages from The Red and the Black, Les Misérables, Madame Bovary, and other classics. Original French text plus English translation on facing pages. 240pp. $5\frac{3}{8}$ x $8\frac{1}{2}$. 0-486-46178-5

WILBUR AND ORVILLE: A Biography of the Wright Brothers, Fred Howard. Definitive, crisply written study tells the full story of the brothers' lives and work. A vividly written biography, unparalleled in scope and color, that also captures the spirit of an extraordinary era. 560pp. $6\frac{1}{8}$ x $9\frac{1}{4}$. 0-486-40297-5

THE ARTS OF THE SAILOR: Knotting, Splicing and Ropework, Hervey Garrett Smith. Indispensable shipboard reference covers tools, basic knots and useful hitches; handsewing and canvas work, more. Over 100 illustrations. Delightful reading for sea lovers. 256pp. $5\frac{3}{8}$ x $8\frac{1}{2}$. 0-486-26440-8

FRANK LLOYD WRIGHT'S FALLINGWATER: The House and Its History, Second, Revised Edition, Donald Hoffmann. A total revision–both in text and illustrations–of the standard document on Fallingwater, the boldest, most personal architectural statement of Wright's mature years, updated with valuable new material from the recently opened Frank Lloyd Wright Archives. "Fascinating"–*The New York Times.* 116 illustrations. 128pp. $9\frac{1}{4}$ x $10\frac{3}{4}$. 0-486-27430-6

PHOTOGRAPHIC SKETCHBOOK OF THE CIVIL WAR, Alexander Gardner. 100 photos taken on field during the Civil War. Famous shots of Manassas Harper's Ferry, Lincoln, Richmond, slave pens, etc. 244pp. $10\frac{5}{8}$ x $8\frac{1}{4}$. 0-486-22731-6

FIVE ACRES AND INDEPENDENCE, Maurice G. Kains. Great back-to-the-land classic explains basics of self-sufficient farming. The one book to get. 95 illustrations. 397pp. $5\frac{3}{8}$ x $8\frac{1}{2}$. 0-486-20974-1

A MODERN HERBAL, Margaret Grieve. Much the fullest, most exact, most useful compilation of herbal material. Gigantic alphabetical encyclopedia, from aconite to zedoary, gives botanical information, medical properties, folklore, economic uses, much else. Indispensable to serious reader. 161 illustrations. 888pp. 6½ x 9¼. 2-vol. set. (Available in U.S. only.)   Vol. I: 0-486-22798-7   Vol. II: 0-486-22799-5

HIDDEN TREASURE MAZE BOOK, Dave Phillips. Solve 34 challenging mazes accompanied by heroic tales of adventure. Evil dragons, people-eating plants, blood-thirsty giants, many more dangerous adversaries lurk at every twist and turn. 34 mazes, stories, solutions. 48pp. 8¼ x 11.   0-486-24566-7

LETTERS OF W. A. MOZART, Wolfgang A. Mozart. Remarkable letters show bawdy wit, humor, imagination, musical insights, contemporary musical world; includes some letters from Leopold Mozart. 276pp. 5⅜ x 8½.   0-486-22859-2

BASIC PRINCIPLES OF CLASSICAL BALLET, Agrippina Vaganova. Great Russian theoretician, teacher explains methods for teaching classical ballet. 118 illustrations. 175pp. 5⅜ x 8½.   0-486-22036-2

THE JUMPING FROG, Mark Twain. Revenge edition. The original story of The Celebrated Jumping Frog of Calaveras County, a hapless French translation, and Twain's hilarious "retranslation" from the French. 12 illustrations. 66pp. 5⅜ x 8½.
0-486-22686-7

BEST REMEMBERED POEMS, Martin Gardner (ed.). The 126 poems in this superb collection of 19th- and 20th-century British and American verse range from Shelley's "To a Skylark" to the impassioned "Renascence" of Edna St. Vincent Millay and to Edward Lear's whimsical "The Owl and the Pussycat." 224pp. 5⅜ x 8½.
0-486-27165-X

COMPLETE SONNETS, William Shakespeare. Over 150 exquisite poems deal with love, friendship, the tyranny of time, beauty's evanescence, death and other themes in language of remarkable power, precision and beauty. Glossary of archaic terms. 80pp. 5³⁄₁₆ x 8¼.   0-486-26686-9

HISTORIC HOMES OF THE AMERICAN PRESIDENTS, Second, Revised Edition, Irvin Haas. A traveler's guide to American Presidential homes, most open to the public, depicting and describing homes occupied by every American President from George Washington to George Bush. With visiting hours, admission charges, travel routes. 175 photographs. Index. 160pp. 8¼ x 11.   0-486-26751-2

THE WIT AND HUMOR OF OSCAR WILDE, Alvin Redman (ed.). More than 1,000 ripostes, paradoxes, wisecracks: Work is the curse of the drinking classes; I can resist everything except temptation; etc. 258pp. 5⅜ x 8½.   0-486-20602-5

SHAKESPEARE LEXICON AND QUOTATION DICTIONARY, Alexander Schmidt. Full definitions, locations, shades of meaning in every word in plays and poems. More than 50,000 exact quotations. 1,485pp. 6½ x 9¼. 2-vol. set.
Vol. 1: 0-486-22726-X   Vol. 2: 0-486-22727-8

SELECTED POEMS, Emily Dickinson. Over 100 best-known, best-loved poems by one of America's foremost poets, reprinted from authoritative early editions. No comparable edition at this price. Index of first lines. 64pp. 5³⁄₁₆ x 8¼. 0-486-26466-1

THE INSIDIOUS DR. FU-MANCHU, Sax Rohmer. The first of the popular mystery series introduces a pair of English detectives to their archnemesis, the diabolical Dr. Fu-Manchu. Flavorful atmosphere, fast-paced action, and colorful characters enliven this classic of the genre. 208pp. 5³⁄₁₆ x 8¼.   0-486-29898-1

MAGIC AND MYSTERY IN TIBET, Madame Alexandra David-Neel. Experiences among lamas, magicians, sages, sorcerers, Bonpa wizards. A true psychic discovery. 32 illustrations. 321pp. 5⅜ x 8½. (Available in U.S. only.) 0-486-22682-4

THE EGYPTIAN BOOK OF THE DEAD, E. A. Wallis Budge. Complete reproduction of Ani's papyrus, finest ever found. Full hieroglyphic text, interlinear transliteration, word-for-word translation, smooth translation. 533pp. 6½ x 9¼.
0-486-21866-X

HISTORIC COSTUME IN PICTURES, Braun & Schneider. Over 1,450 costumed figures in clearly detailed engravings–from dawn of civilization to end of 19th century. Captions. Many folk costumes. 256pp. 8⅜ x 11¾. 0-486-23150-X

MATHEMATICS FOR THE NONMATHEMATICIAN, Morris Kline. Detailed, college-level treatment of mathematics in cultural and historical context, with numerous exercises. Recommended Reading Lists. Tables. Numerous figures. 641pp. 5⅜ x 8½. 0-486-24823-2

PROBABILISTIC METHODS IN THE THEORY OF STRUCTURES, Isaac Elishakoff. Well-written introduction covers the elements of the theory of probability from two or more random variables, the reliability of such multivariable structures, the theory of random function, Monte Carlo methods of treating problems incapable of exact solution, and more. Examples. 502pp. 5⅜ x 8½. 0-486-40691-1

THE RIME OF THE ANCIENT MARINER, Gustave Doré, S. T. Coleridge. Doré's finest work; 34 plates capture moods, subtleties of poem. Flawless full-size reproductions printed on facing pages with authoritative text of poem. "Beautiful. Simply beautiful."–*Publisher's Weekly.* 77pp. 9¼ x 12. 0-486-22305-1

SCULPTURE: Principles and Practice, Louis Slobodkin. Step-by-step approach to clay, plaster, metals, stone; classical and modern. 253 drawings, photos. 255pp. 8⅛ x 11. 0-486-22960-2

THE INFLUENCE OF SEA POWER UPON HISTORY, 1660–1783, A. T. Mahan. Influential classic of naval history and tactics still used as text in war colleges. First paperback edition. 4 maps. 24 battle plans. 640pp. 5⅜ x 8½. 0-486-25509-3

THE STORY OF THE TITANIC AS TOLD BY ITS SURVIVORS, Jack Winocour (ed.). What it was really like. Panic, despair, shocking inefficiency, and a little heroism. More thrilling than any fictional account. 26 illustrations. 320pp. 5⅜ x 8½.
0-486-20610-6

ONE TWO THREE . . . INFINITY: Facts and Speculations of Science, George Gamow. Great physicist's fascinating, readable overview of contemporary science: number theory, relativity, fourth dimension, entropy, genes, atomic structure, much more. 128 illustrations. Index. 352pp. 5⅜ x 8½. 0-486-25664-2

DALÍ ON MODERN ART: The Cuckolds of Antiquated Modern Art, Salvador Dalí. Influential painter skewers modern art and its practitioners. Outrageous evaluations of Picasso, Cézanne, Turner, more. 15 renderings of paintings discussed. 44 calligraphic decorations by Dalí. 96pp. 5⅜ x 8½. (Available in U.S. only.) 0-486-29220-7

ANTIQUE PLAYING CARDS: A Pictorial History, Henry René D'Allemagne. Over 900 elaborate, decorative images from rare playing cards (14th–20th centuries): Bacchus, death, dancing dogs, hunting scenes, royal coats of arms, players cheating, much more. 96pp. 9¼ x 12¼. 0-486-29265-7

LIGHT AND SHADE: A Classic Approach to Three-Dimensional Drawing, Mrs. Mary P. Merrifield. Handy reference clearly demonstrates principles of light and shade by revealing effects of common daylight, sunshine, and candle or artificial light on geometrical solids. 13 plates. 64pp. 5⅜ x 8½.   0-486-44143-1

ASTROLOGY AND ASTRONOMY: A Pictorial Archive of Signs and Symbols, Ernst and Johanna Lehner. Treasure trove of stories, lore, and myth, accompanied by more than 300 rare illustrations of planets, the Milky Way, signs of the zodiac, comets, meteors, and other astronomical phenomena. 192pp. 8⅜ x 11.

0-486-43981-X

JEWELRY MAKING: Techniques for Metal, Tim McCreight. Easy-to-follow instructions and carefully executed illustrations describe tools and techniques, use of gems and enamels, wire inlay, casting, and other topics. 72 line illustrations and diagrams. 176pp. 8¼ x 10⅞.   0-486-44043-5

MAKING BIRDHOUSES: Easy and Advanced Projects, Gladstone Califf. Easy-to-follow instructions include diagrams for everything from a one-room house for bluebirds to a forty-two-room structure for purple martins. 56 plates; 4 figures. 80pp. 8¾ x 6⅜.   0-486-44183-0

LITTLE BOOK OF LOG CABINS: How to Build and Furnish Them, William S. Wicks. Handy how-to manual, with instructions and illustrations for building cabins in the Adirondack style, fireplaces, stairways, furniture, beamed ceilings, and more. 102 line drawings. 96pp. 8¾ x 6⅜.   0-486-44259-4

THE SEASONS OF AMERICA PAST, Eric Sloane. From "sugaring time" and strawberry picking to Indian summer and fall harvest, a whole year's activities described in charming prose and enhanced with 79 of the author's own illustrations. 160pp. 8¼ x 11.   0-486-44220-9

THE METROPOLIS OF TOMORROW, Hugh Ferriss. Generous, prophetic vision of the metropolis of the future, as perceived in 1929. Powerful illustrations of towering structures, wide avenues, and rooftop parks—all features in many of today's modern cities. 59 illustrations. 144pp. 8¼ x 11.   0-486-43727-2

THE PATH TO ROME, Hilaire Belloc. This 1902 memoir abounds in lively vignettes from a vanished time, recounting a pilgrimage on foot across the Alps and Apennines in order to "see all Europe which the Christian Faith has saved." 77 of the author's original line drawings complement his sparkling prose. 272pp. 5⅜ x 8½.

0-486-44001-X

THE HISTORY OF RASSELAS: Prince of Abissinia, Samuel Johnson. Distinguished English writer attacks eighteenth-century optimism and man's unrealistic estimates of what life has to offer. 112pp. 5⅜ x 8½.   0-486-44094-X

A VOYAGE TO ARCTURUS, David Lindsay. A brilliant flight of pure fancy, where wild creatures crowd the fantastic landscape and demented torturers dominate victims with their bizarre mental powers. 272pp. 5⅜ x 8½.   0-486-44198-9